IESE CITIES IN MOTION:
INTERNATIONAL URBAN BEST PRACTICES

CITIES AND MOBILITY & TRANSPORTATION

TOWARDS THE NEXT GENERATION OF URBAN MOBILITY

VOLUME 2

PROF. PASCUAL BERRONE
PROF. JOAN ENRIC RICART COSTA
ANA ISABEL DUCH T-FIGUERAS

Preface to the Book Series

"IESE CITIES IN MOTION:
International urban best practices"

The world is experiencing the largest increase in urban growth in history. Today, more than half of the world's population lives in cities and it is forecast that the percentage of urban residents in the global population will increase to almost 70% by 2050. This unprecedented growth in urbanization has the potential to bring significant benefits for citizens, such as new jobs and well-being, along with overall economic growth. However, rapid urbanization also multiplies the number, size and complexity of the challenges faced by cities, such as increasing pressure on scarce resources, greater demand for basic infrastructure and public services, as well as greater socioeconomic inequality.

Cities must be able to solve economic, social and environmental problems simultaneously, in all cases with the aim of improving the welfare and quality of life of their residents. In their search for sustainable, equitable, connected and innovative city models, municipal leaders around the world look at the experiences of other cities to get ideas and study best practices. Although there is no "one size fits all" solution, this book series aims to help city managers in their endeavors to create urban areas that are environmentally, economically and socially sustainable. With this objective, this series will examine some of the actions, projects and initiatives that have had the best results in cities internationally, so that other cities around the world can build on the most successful approaches and adapt them to their local realities and needs.

The book series is structured on the basis of the IESE Cities in Motion model, which includes an innovative approach to the governance of cities and a new urban model for the 21st century based on 10 key areas or dimensions: human capital, social cohesion, the economy, public management, governance, mobility and transportation, the environment, urban planning, technology and international outreach. Each volume in this series provides an overview of the main challenges regarding a specific dimension and exhibits some of the most successful initiatives and actions that have been adopted in regard to that area in different cities around the world. Despite the fact that each area is covered in a separate volume of its own, all the key areas must be seen as different parts of a system that works as one. All the dimensions are interconnected and actions in one area affect other areas at the same time. Therefore, the available resources must be shared and managed together in order to achieve sustainable, lively, healthy and safe cities.

With this book series, we aim to contribute to the debate on smart urban governance by developing valuable ideas and innovative tools that can lead to smarter and more sustainable cities, while promoting real change at the local level and improving people's quality of life. We believe that current urban challenges are not only problems to be solved, but also opportunities to be exploited.

Prior volumes of this series:

Vol. 1: *Cities and the Environment: The Challenge of Becoming Green and Sustainable,* CreateSpace, 2016.

See, **"Greening Up in the City"**. Available at: http://www.amazon.com/dp/1523965789.

"Responsible for the vast majority of the world's energy use and greenhouse gas emissions, urban areas are also the main contributors to air, noise, water, and land pollution. Moreover, cities generate large quantities of waste, are voracious consumers of natural resources, and they are particularly vulnerable to natural disasters and climate change. Given the current rates of urbanization, the environmental impacts of cities are of urgent concern. This first volume of the series focuses on the effects of urbanization on our planet, analyzing the main environmental challenges that city governments face, and offering a catalog of international urban best practices on environmental issues."

Contents

Preface...iii

1. Introduction...1

2. Urban Mobility Trends and Challenges...5

    2.1 Traffic Congestion, Long Commuting Times and Parking Difficulties 7

    2.2 Traffic Accidents and Safety 10

    2.3 Environmental Impacts and Energy Consumption of Mobility.....................11

    2.4 Public Transport Inadequacy and Spatial Social Divisions 14

3. **New Urban Mobility Patterns: Smart Solutions and Best Practices..............23**

    3.1 People Mobility...27

        3.1.1 Walking and Cycling...27

        3.1.2 Sharing Mobility Systems...29

            a. Bike-sharing...30

            b. Car-sharing 37

            c. Ride-sharing and Ride-hailing...38

        3.1.3 Local Public Transport...47

        3.1.4 Integrated Multi-modal Transport and Smarter Mobility Services.....55

            a. Smart Ticketing...56

            b. Integrated Travel Information..59

    3.2 Transport Demand Management 61

        3.2.1 Real-time Traffic Management..61

        3.2.2 Parking Management: Smart Parking..64

    3.3 Urban Freight and City Logistics 68

    3.4 Green Mobility and Low Emissions Zones 73

        3.4.1 Clean and Energy Efficient Vehicles 74

        3.4.2 Congestion Charges and Low Emission Zones....................................76

    3.5 Other Mobility Solutions of the Future...80

            a. Autonomous vehicles (AVs)..81

4. Concluding Remarks...83

5. References...87

6. Appendix I: Additional Resources 95

7. Appendix II: Cities in Motion Index –
   Mobility and Transportation Dimension...97

1. Introduction

Mobility is crucial to the social and economic development of cities: it provides access to jobs and schools, eases people's contact to services and information, delivers products, facilitates business, maintains security, allows socialization, improves access to health services and gives a sense of personal freedom to individuals around the world. In other words, urban mobility impacts the "livability" and functioning of cities. Therefore, **the better and more efficient connectivity and accessibility in cities are, the greater the wellbeing of people will be**.

However, under a business-as-usual scenario, urban mobility also poses important challenges to cities in both developing and developed countries. These challenges range from environmental pressures - such as increasing greenhouse gas (GHG) emissions, air and noise pollution and energy consumption - to traffic congestion, traffic accidents, health issues and deepening social divisions. In order to successfully cope with these issues, city managers around the world need to recognize their importance and generate new ideas and strategies to improve, reinvent and redesign existing urban mobility systems. The choices city administrators make today about mobility and transportation will significantly determine the sustainability of urban areas and the quality of life of the citizens in the future.

Today, three central elements are driving urban mobility developments: 1) a rising demand for urban mobility; 2) a change in people's behavior patterns and preferences; and 3) technological advances. First, the unprecedented increase in the world's urban population, along with rising Gross Domestic Products (GDPs) and incomes per capita in most parts of the world, is intensifying the demand for urban mobility as never before. Today, **around 10 billion trips are made every day in urban areas globally - representing some 64% of all travel made - and the total amount of urban kilometers travelled worldwide is expected to almost triple by 2050** (Rode et al., 2014; Van-Audenhove, Korniichuk, Dauby and Pourbaix, 2014). Also, in 2010 the unthinkable amount of €6,400 billion was spent on the transport of people and goods globally – four times more than in 1970 and outplacing global GDP growth (Cornet, Mohr, Weig, Zerlin and Hein, 2012). Mobility now accounts for 13% of worldwide GDP. This rising urban mobility demand is putting a severe strain on the current world's urban infrastructure, especially in developing and emerging countries, where most of the remaining urban growth will take place.

Second, along with a rising demand for urban mobility, **cities are experiencing a change in consumers' mobility patterns, preferences and behaviors**. Urban dwellers are asking for more convenient mobility options. A survey by Deloitte found that young urban inhabitants – the so-called Generation Y or millennials – are not as devoted to personal vehicles as previous generations and are more interested in alternative modes of transportation, such as shared mobility services (Deloitte, 2014).[1] For instance, millennials in the United States, the country with the highest car ownership rate in the world, are 23% less interested in owning a car than the previous generation (Bouton, et al., 2015). Additionally, citizens are becoming more concerned about the environmental footprint of their actions and are demanding greener and more sustainable mobility options. According to the previously mentioned survey, the majority of the Gen-Y consumers, especially in Western countries, think that they will be utilizing an alternative engine in five years and they are willing to pay more for it

---

[1] The survey covered 23,000 consumers in 19 countries around the world (Deloitte, 2014).

(Deloitte, 2014).[2] Therefore, new mobility behaviors and new preferences are leading the way.

And last but not least, **technological advances and innovations are reshaping the game, changing existing urban transport systems**. Information and Communication Technologies (hereinafter ICTs) have considerably improved existing urban mobility systems through more efficient transport management, travel information and mobility options. In particular, a combination of smartphone technologies and geo-positioning systems (GPS) has enabled real time transport information, updated network maps and improved service quality. This will considerably increase the share of trips that are multi-modal, as well as the development of new business models and ways to move around in cities.

All of these forces are driving a new era in mobility.

*****

Following this brief introduction, Section 2 discusses how urban mobility has evolved over the centuries, as well as current and future trends, and the challenges of urban mobility and transportation. Section 3 highlights international urban best practices in mobility and transportation and assesses different solutions and strategies for achieving a sustainable mobility system in cities. The last section of the book offers some concluding remarks.

*****

---

[2] This trend may be reverse in developing countries, where car ownership is still highly desired and emerging middle-class populations are driving growth in car ownerships.

2. Urban Mobility Trends and Challenges

Many aspects of today's urban transport challenges are linked to the reign of the automobile as the preferred means of transport, which has led to urban sprawl, lower urban density and longer distances travelled. Different factors, such as investments in road infrastructures and higher incomes per capita have eased this trend. However, cities have not always been car-centered designed.

Before analyzing some of the current trends and challenges of urban mobility, this section is going to briefly explore how urban mobility has changed over the past decades and centuries.

How has the concept of Urban Mobility evolved?

The development of urban areas cannot be considered separate from urban mobility and transportation. In fact, the progress of human societies has always been associated with moving around. However, urban mobility has advanced and changed dramatically over the centuries. A combination of different demographic patterns, economic growth, societal changes and, more recently, advances in technology and transport policies have driven this evolution (Jones, 2014; Rode, et al., 2014).

Pre-industrial cities differed significantly from today's cities. In general, they were small settlements, most of them compacted and surrounded by a wall, with a small percentage of the total population living in towns. Means of movement and transportation in pre-industrial cities were slow and inefficient. The main way to move around was on foot. Therefore, to take advantage of proximity, houses were built closely together along irregular and narrow streets.

The Industrial Revolution of the 18th and 19th centuries triggered the movement of a great number of people from the countryside to urban areas, resulting in an urban revolution and giving rise to the *industrial city*. Industrial cities were larger and more densely populated than pre-industrial cities and, as their populations grew, they had to adapt and design new means of mobility. A good example is the development of inland canal systems in many Western countries in the 18th century, which reduced costs for freight movement and stimulated the early stages of the Industrial Revolution (Jones, 2014). Shortly after, in the beginning of the 19th century, the invention of steam-powered technology enabled the rise of the railway industry, facilitating the movement of people to cities and/or around their countries. By and large, industrial cities were still focused on a city center, where trolleys and railroads converged.

At the beginning of the 20th century, with the evolution of the mass production industry, the car industry emerged and the *modern city* was born. As automobiles became more common, cities had to be redesigned and rebuilt around the motor vehicle: high-capacity roads, wide streets and fast highways began to pervade cities. Urban sprawl, growing incomes, the influence and rise of the automobile industry, and large investments in roads were all factors that contributed to the car-centered city. The automobile came to be seen as the ideal solution for urban mobility and, accordingly, cities began designing urban centers and their suburbs to facilitate car traffic. As a result, the dominance of the private motorized transport during the 20th century greatly influenced the configuration of contemporary cities in terms of form, structure and function.

Urban mobility in the 21ˢᵗ century

In recent decades, due to the increasing number of people moving from rural to urban areas, modern industrial cities have significantly grown in size. Road transport infrastructures have expanded in cities around the world, generally covering 10-25% of urban areas today. In the US, this can reach up to 45% (Breithaupt, 2015).

Although it is true that the automobile offers many advantages, such as increased convenience, comfort and speed, its dominance can also have serious effects on citizens' quality of life. Externalities of automobiles may include overcrowding, congestion, high consumption of energy, environmental costs and a lack of walkability, especially in cities with a high level of population density. Therefore, providing additional road capacity might not be the solution.

The negative impacts, trends and challenges of contemporary urban mobility are outlined below.

***

2.1 Traffic Congestion, Long Commuting Times and Parking Difficulties

Cities have grown so rapidly in recent decades that the supply of transport infrastructures has usually not been able to keep up with the associated rise in urban mobility demand. This imbalance between supply and demand has resulted in huge levels of traffic congestion, making mobility – especially in peak hours – very difficult. **In a business-as-usual scenario, by 2050, the average time an urban dweller will spend in traffic jams will be 106 hours per year, twice the current rate** (Van-Audenhove, et al., 2014).

According to TomTom Traffic Index, Mexico City was the most congested city in 2015, followed by Bangkok and Istanbul.[3] Moreover, TomTom data reveals that traffic congestion almost doubles journey times during the evening rush hours. For instance, Bangkok's congestion level in 2015 increased from an average of 57% up to 114% in the evening peak (TomTom International BV, 2016).

Table 1: TomTom traffic congestion index in 2015

World rank	City (Country)	Congestion level (%)
1	Mexico City (Mexico)	59%
2	Bangkok (Thailand)	57%
3	Istanbul (Turkey)	50%
4	Rio de Janeiro (Brazil)	47%
5	Moscow (Russia)	44%
6	Bucharest (Romania)	43%
7	Salvador (Brazil)	43%
8	Recife (Brazil)	43%
9	Chengdu (China)	41%
10	Los Angeles (USA)	41%

Source: Based on TomTom Traffic Index (2016)

High levels of road congestion have important economic and social consequences for cities. On one hand, urban gridlocks produce losses in productivity and economic efficiency. **Congestion costs are estimated to be as much as 1% to 5% of GDP as a result of lost time, wasted fuel and/or increased cost of doing business** (Bouton, et al., 2015; Floater and Rode, 2014). These costs are often higher in developing and emerging countries with rapidly growing cities and limited resources and capabilities. For instance, the costs of congestion are estimated to reflect 3.4% of the

---

[3] The TomTom Traffic Index covers 295 cities in 50 countries (TomTom International BV, 2016).

GDP of Buenos Aires and Dakar; 2.6% for Mexico City; some 4% for Cairo; and 7.8% for Sao Paulo (World Bank, 2002; Zenghelis and Stern, 2015). On a regional level, mobility in cities accounts for roughly 3.5% of Latin America's annual GDP, while in Europe this reflects just 1% of the GDP (European Commission, 2011; Thomson and Bull, 2002). Lastly, some studies have estimated the overall costs of congestion in currency units, finding annual congestion costs as high as $23.2 billion in the city of Los Angeles, $11.7 billion in Paris and $8.5 billion in London in 2013 (Cebr, 2014). In Cairo, the costs of congestion reflected $8.0 billion in 2010 (World Bank, 2012).

On the other hand, traffic congestion often results from long-distance commuting, which has social consequences. Congestion and lost time resulting from extensive commuting not only has negative effects on the well-being of the population, but it also has social consequences for individual commuters and society as a whole (Box 1).

BOX 1. Long- distance commuters get divorced more often

According to a doctoral thesis from Umea University, the risk of marital separation is 40% higher among long-distance commuters than among other people (Sandow, 2011). The study, which covers more than two million Swedes who were married or cohabiting in 2000, shows that although commuting to work can be beneficial in terms of income and career opportunities, it also entails less time for family and friends, can lead to stress and health problems and can jeopardize relationships. Therefore, long-distance commuting can have negative social consequences for individuals.

Lastly, since most vehicles spend some 90-95% of the day parked, the demand for parking – particularly in city centers – has also increased substantially. Traffic congestion and parking are also interrelated since it is estimated that **as much as 30% of city-center traffic comes from people trying to find a parking space** at any given time (Shoup, 2006). This issue is also of critical importance for the transportation of goods, since many delivery vehicles need a place to park to drop off their cargo.

2.2 Traffic Accidents and Safety

Rising traffic in urban areas is directly linked with a higher number of road traffic accidents and traffic-related injuries and fatalities. According to the World Health Organization (WHO), road traffic accidents are the eighth leading cause of death globally and current trends suggest that they will become the fifth leading cause of death by 2030. **Worldwide, about 1.24 million people die each year on the roads and up to 50 million people endure non-fatal injuries** (World Health Organization, 2013). In 2010, the average road traffic fatality rate of low and middle-income countries, 18.3 and 20.1, respectively, was nearly twice that of developed countries, which was 8.7 (UN-Habitat, 2013; World Health Organization, 2013). Moreover, road traffic deaths are projected to double from 1.2 million in 2011 to 2.4 million in 2030 (Floater and Rode, 2014). Therefore, traffic accidents remain an important public health issue to be addressed.

Of the abovementioned deaths and injuries on the world's roads, about 50% of deaths and 75% of injuries occurred in urban areas (Floater and Rode, 2014; World Bank, 2002). Due to the projected increase in volume of urban traffic in future decades, it is estimated that the number of urban traffic fatalities will rise 30% by 2025 (UITP, 2012). This issue is remarkably important for developing countries, in particular cities in the Middle-East and North-Africa (MENA) region, Sub-Saharan Africa and in developing Asia. These regions will account for 85% of urban traffic fatalities by 2025, according to estimates (UITP, 2012).

Therefore, implementing strategies, road-safety plans and action programs to reduce traffic accidents is critical, both in developed and developing countries. The city of Copenhagen, for instance, has the safest urban mobility system in the world, with only 4.1 traffic deaths per million citizens (Van-Audenhove, et al., 2014). This is a result of a number of programs and strategies that take a holistic approach to urban mobility, resulting in a safer and more efficient transportation system.

***

2.3 Environmental Impacts and Energy Consumption of Mobility

As illustrated in the first book volume of this series, *Cities and the Environment*, urban areas are major contributors to global GHG emissions, as well as air and noise pollution (Berrone, Ricart, and Duch, 2016).[4] As the pace of urbanization accelerates, the demand for urban mobility also rises, exacerbating its environmental impact.

Cities are particularly exposed to GHG emissions and pollution, due to the dominance of automobiles as the main mode of transport and the large number of vehicles in high-density areas. The current interdependence between oil and non-renewable fossil fuels and transport magnifies current environmental challenges. In fact, 90% of transport fuels are oil-based and 50% of oil produced worldwide is consumed by the transport sector (UITP, 2015b).

Additionally, the transport sector accounts for between 20% and 30% of global energy use and it has been the fastest growing source of carbon emissions in the world, and a major cause of climate change, global warming and rising sea levels (UN-Habitat, 2013). CO_2 is the main transport-related GHG and, worldwide, CO_2 emissions from the mobility and transport sector increased by 85% between 1973 and 2007 (UN-Habitat, 2013). Today, **urban transport generates approximately 40% of all GHG emissions**. In

---

[4] Due to the fact that most environmental challenges faced by cities are analyzed in the book volume Cities and the Environment, this section covers only the environmental challenges and impacts of the mobility and transport sectors in urban areas.

2010, mobility in urban areas accounted for about 2,300 megatons of CO_2, which is equivalent in weight to more than 338 million African elephants or more than 15 million blue whales (Replogle, 2014; United Nations, 2014).[5] This represents almost one quarter of carbon emissions from all parts of the transport sector.

Under a business-as-usual scenario, energy use and GHG emissions from the land transport sector are expected to increase nearly 50% by 2030 and more than 80% by 2050, as compared with 2009 (UN, 2014). In addition, some studies estimate that urban mobility systems will use 17.3% of the planet's biocapacity by 2050, which reflects about five times more than they used in 1990 (Van-Audenhove, et al., 2014). However, if proper actions are put in place in cities, such as expanding public transportation, walking and cycling, some 1,700 megatons of annual CO_2 could be eliminated by 2050 – a 40% reduction (Figure 1).

Figure 1: Scenarios for pollution from urban transportation

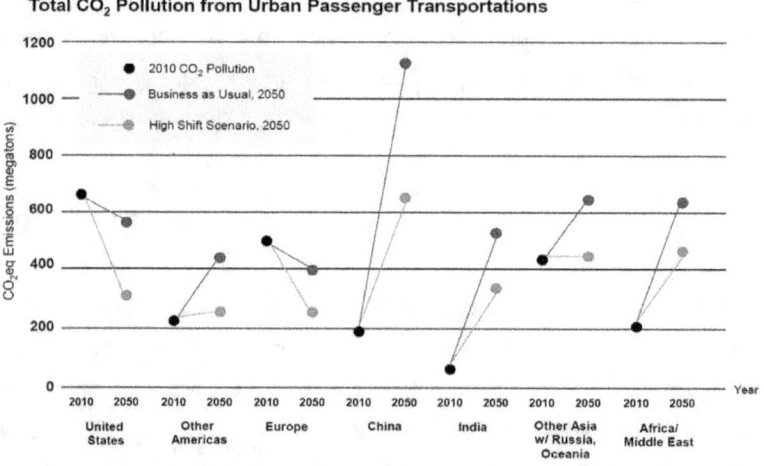

Total CO_2 Pollution from Urban Passenger Transportations

Source: ITDP and University of California, Davis (2014)

[5] A megaton is 1 million (1,000,000) metric tons. A male African elephant weighs some 6.8 metric tons, so a megaton is the equivalent of more than 147,000 African elephants. Similarly, a blue whale can weigh up to 146 metric tons, so a megaton is the weight of some 6,800 blue whales (Mooney, 2015).

As shown in Figure 2, cities in industrialized countries account for most per capita transport-related CO_2 emissions. In particular, cities in North America occupy the top spots on the list. However, in upcoming years, close to 90% of the increase in overall transport-related CO_2 emissions is expected to take place in developing countries, particularly in emerging economy megacities (UNCSD, 2012).

Figure 2: Per capita emissions of CO_2 from passenger transport in selected cities

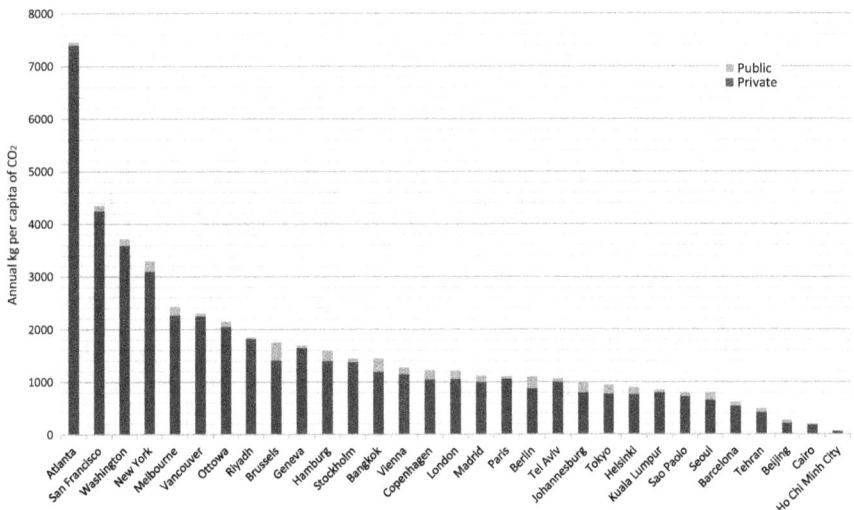

Source: Prepared by the authors based on Kenworthy Jr. (2003)

Additionally, GHG emissions in cities entail increasing exposure to smog and air and noise pollution by city dwellers, which presents serious public concerns. As mentioned in the volume 1 of this series, the WHO estimated that in 2012 around 7 million people died worldwide as a result of air pollution exposure, with a significant share being a result of urban transport (WHO, 2014).

The abovementioned trends of CO_2 emissions and energy consumption are unsustainable and we must identify a solution. New strategies to change current mobility patterns and elude climate change are crucial for reverting this tendency. According to some estimates, **the world's 724 largest cities could reduce GHG emissions by up to 1.5 billion tons of CO_2 annually by 2030 primarily through transformative changes in transportation systems** (New Climate Economy, 2014). In this regard, some cities are making noteworthy improvements in relation to improving transport efficiency that will be further exhibited in Section 3.

***

2.4 Public Transport Inadequacy and Spatial Social Divisions

Conventionally, there are three classes of urban travel: non-motorized transport (cycling and walking), private motorized transport and public transport. Due to the lack of adequate infrastructures, the main mode of transport in many cities in developing countries is still non-motorized transport, primarily walking and cycling (Figure 3).

Figure 3: Urban travel modal shares (as percentages of all trips) in selected cities

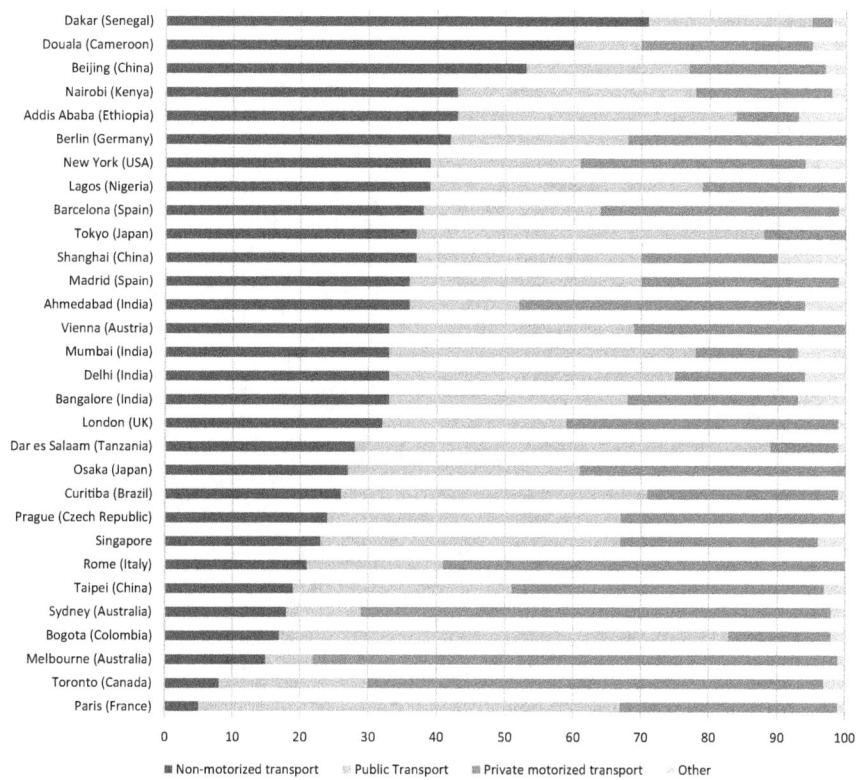

Note: data for years from 2006 to 2011, depending on the city and the source

Source: Prepared by the authors based on LTA Academy (2011) and UN-Habitat (2013)

Traditionally, it has been thought that economic growth is positively and strongly correlated with the use of private cars. However, as shown in Figure 4 below, this only applies to the North American pattern. There are other models of modal share that suggest that an increase in GDP per capita can also go along with other transport models that rely less on the private car.

Figure 4: GDP per capita vs. modal share of motorized private mode.

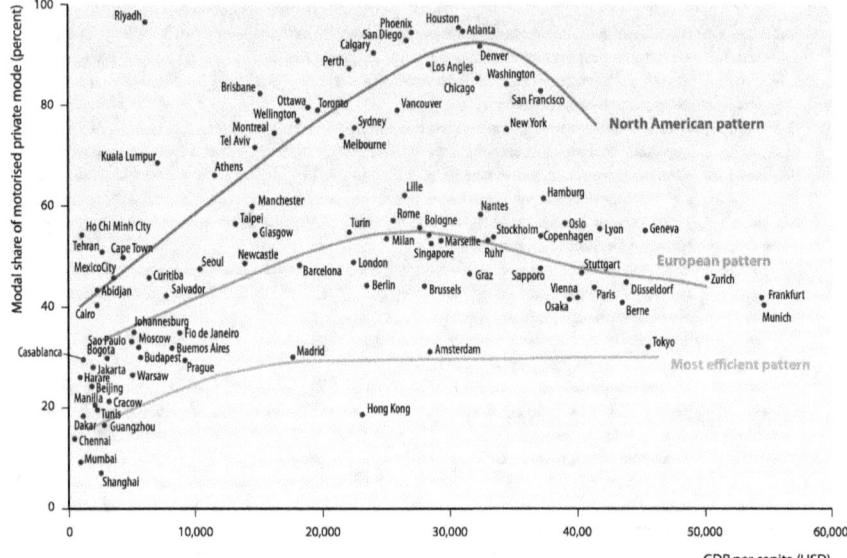

Source: UITP, 2006 (Courtesy of SYSTRA)

One of those options is public transport. **Public transportation permits the mobility of a higher number of people with fewer vehicles, less energy consumption and in less space**. Table 2 shows that cities with a modal share of public transport, cycling and walking above 55% produce, on average, about 2.4 tons less CO_2 from passenger transport per capita per year than cities where the modal share of private motorized modes is above 75% (UITP, 2009). Therefore, in the context of rapid urbanization that we are currently facing, the provision of an efficient and high-capacity public transport system has an important role to play in sustainable urban mobility.

Table 2: CO_2 emissions from passenger transport vs. modal split

Modal share of public transport, walking and cycling	Average CO_2 emissions (kg. per capita per year)	Examples of cities
Less than 25%	3130 kg	Houston, Chicago Melbourne
Between 25% and 40%	974 kg	Glasgow, Manchester, Lille, Nantes
Between 40% and 55%	953 kg	Madrid, London, Copenhagen, Paris, Hamburg
Above 55%	735 kg	Berlin, Tokyo, Singapore, Krakow, Hong Kong

Source: UITP (2009)

Local public transport includes: road transport (buses, Bus Rapid Transit (hereinafter BRT)), rail modes (metro, light rail, tramway, train), ferryboats or other less conventional means such as cable cars. However, the optimal urban public transport system will depend on the characteristics of the urban area and the density level of the city – i.e., if the city's population is spread out uniformly or, on the contrary, it has very compacted, high-density areas (Figures 5.a and 5.b).

Figure 5.a: Percentage of public transport mode vs. population density in selected cities

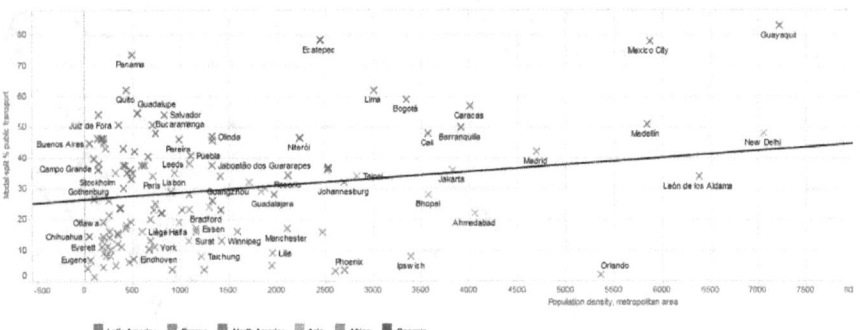

Source: BRT Data (2015)

Figure 5.b: Urban density vs modal split in selected cities

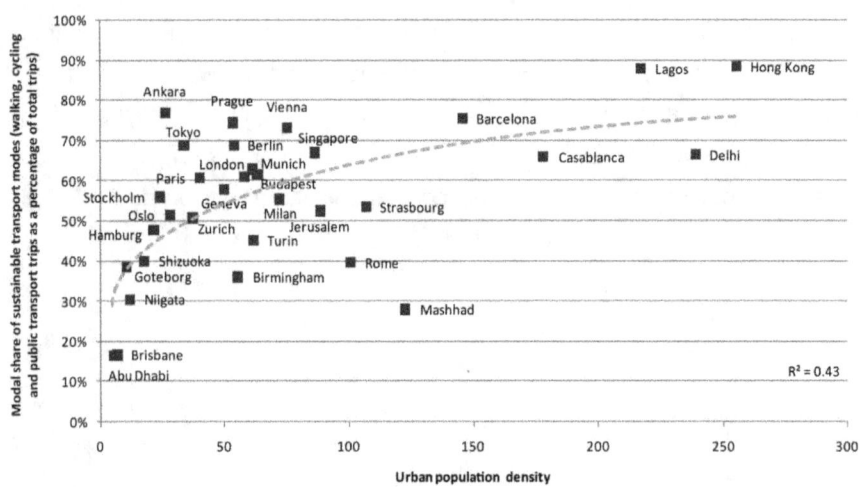

Source: UITP (2015a)

The role and penetration of public transport in cities around the world differs extensively from one city to another. **In 2005 only 16% all urban transport trips worldwide were made by some form of public transport.** Regionally, public transport accounts for some 45% of all urban trips in Eastern Europe and Asia. Yet only 10-20% of trips in Western Europe were made in public transport and less than 5% in Latin America and Sub-Saharan Africa (UN-Habitat, 2013). In fact, in developing countries informal transport is still deeply rooted, accounting for 50% of all motorized trips and 15% of those related to employment (Mbeche, 2013).

Metros are one of the most widely-used forms of public transportation around the world. By the end of 2013, 148 cities in the world had a metro system, with close to 540 lines, with approximately 9,000 metro stations carrying over 150 million passengers per day (UITP, 2014). Two-thirds of the world's metro systems are located in Asia and Europe. Tokyo is the city that carries more passengers in its network, with close to 3.3 billion passenger trips per year. Shanghai has the world's longest network, with more than 500 km. of infrastructure (Figure 6, UITP, 2014).

Figure 6: World's main metro networks by region

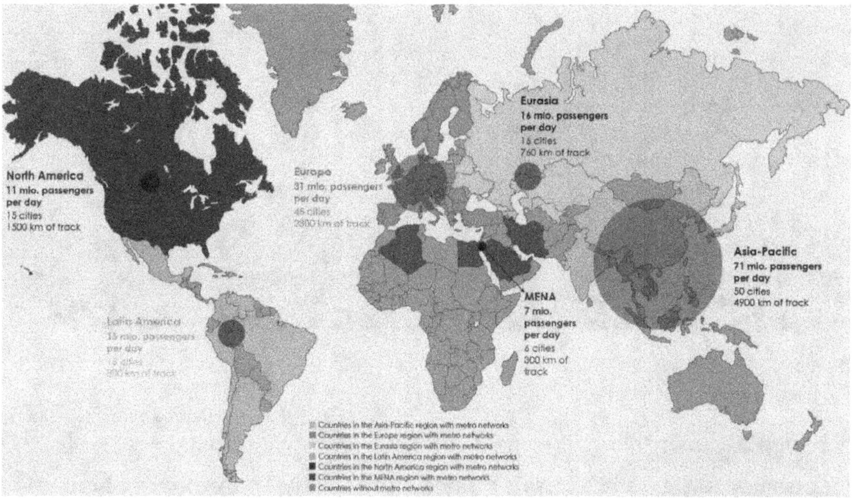

Source: UITP (2014)

Bus rapid transit or BRT systems are a more recently-introduced mass transit approach. As of June 2016, 204 cities on all continents have implemented BRT systems, accounting for 5,333 km. of BRT lanes and transporting an estimated 33 million passengers per day (BRT Data, 2016). Latin America is the region with the largest number of cities using BRT systems, with 67 cities accounting for 32% of the total, followed by Asia (Figure 7).

Figure 7: World's main BRT systems per country.

1. PANORAMA OF **LENGTH (KM)** PER COUNTRY

5 km — 833 km

| 33,294,692 PASSENGER/DAY | 204 CITIES | 418 CORRIDORS | 5,333 km TOTAL LENGTH |

Source: BRTA Data (2016)

Despite its importance, the main problem of public transport is the lack of integration between different modes of mobility. Therefore, as discussed in Section 3, integration within the public transport system and with other modes of transport is a key challenge in this area.

Spatial inequalities

Urban mobility is not only essential for economic development, it is also a way to socialize and access opportunities. **Social and income inequalities are profoundly linked to the spatial arrangements of many cities.** Some social groups, such as people with reduced mobility, lower income groups, school students and senior citizens, face obstacles in accessing many parts of the cities where they live. Therefore, barriers to accessibility are another consequence of negative urban mobility policies, which are aggravated by urban sprawl, personal motorized transport and spatial segregation in suburbs.

The preservation and enhancement of equal accessibility to all and the promotion of social equity, minimizing social exclusion, involve mobility challenges in urban areas, particularly in rapidly urbanizing developing countries. Well-integrated public transportation is a necessary condition for meeting key goals.

***

3. New Urban Mobility Patterns: Smart Solutions and Best Practices

As countries and cities develop, they undergo different urbanization and modernization transitions that may result in very heterogeneous mobility systems among cities at different stages of development and maturity. The strategies needed in a city that already has basic services for traffic - such as street lights, pedestrian crossings, etc. - may differ greatly from the solutions required in a city in a developing country that lacks street lights, walk paths and has chaotic traffic, which demands much more basic mobility infrastructures. Additionally, each city has different urban forms and

Traffic in Dhaka (Bangladesh) vs. Traffic in Barcelona (Spain)

Photos: Flickr/~Pyb and Pixabay/CC0

physical landscapes, as well as diverse socio-economic and demographic pressures. As a result of all these factors, each city requires different strategies in order to overcome its specific local mobility challenges.

However, **taking into account the different realities, cities also face many similar mobility challenges and opportunities, and can learn from the experiences of others**. For instance, cities in emerging countries with underdeveloped mobility systems, which are still in evolution, have the opportunity to design sustainable mobility systems without repeating the same mistakes made by developed countries.

The range of strategies and technological solutions that can be implemented to address urban mobility challenges are extensive and diverse. Recent changes in urban mobility no longer follow traditional patterns of motorization and local administrators need to adopt and support an increasing number of alternatives modes. In fact, many city planners around the world have already put in place different initiatives in order to increase the number of mobility options in cities. For instance, there has been a renewed interest and investment in rail-based public transport systems and building BRT systems, especially in developing countries (Jones, 2014). In addition, expanding walkable neighborhoods and increasing public green spaces have also become priorities for urban managers. Not only that, but new clean energy modes of transport are being developed, adjusting to people's changing preferences towards the use of more sustainable and environmentally-friendly modes of transport. Lastly, the current wave of digitalization is allowing cities to enter a new era of technology-based connected mobility solutions, with computer-aided travelling solutions (e.g. GPS) and advanced traffic management systems.

This section does not attempt to cover all of the existing urban mobility solutions and strategies, but to highlight some of the latest, most innovative and sustainable urban transport solutions. Figure 8 shows the adoption of different mobility solutions in recent decades, as well as the number of cities adopting these solutions. A combination of new technologies with new operating modes, such as bike-sharing and car-sharing, are deeply altering solutions for mobility and transportation in today's cities.

Figure 8: Cities adopting different sustainable transport solutions

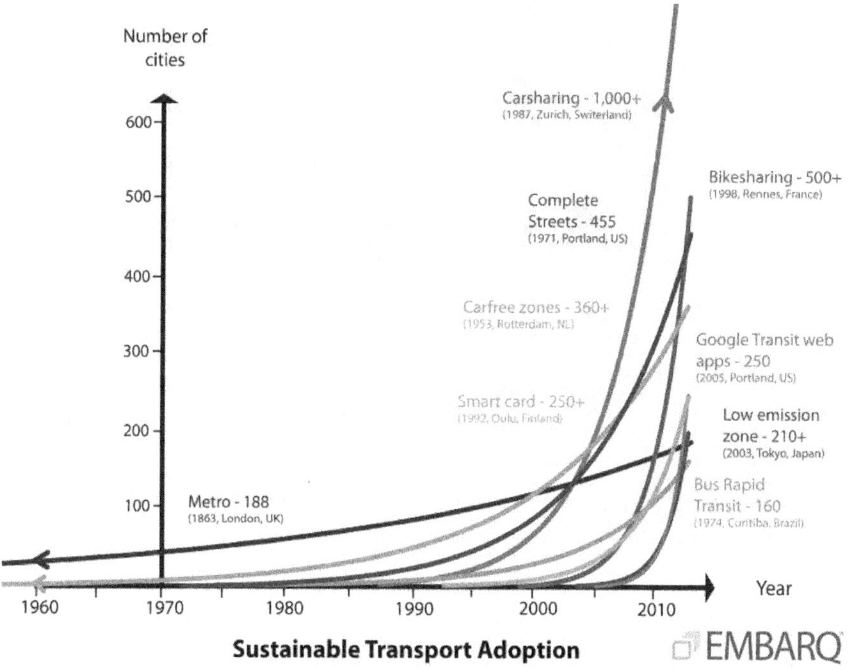

Sustainable Transport Adoption   EMBARQ

Source: World Resource Institute, EMBARQ, 2013

As mentioned in other volumes of the book series, a number of changes are enabling groundbreaking transformations in the way cities operate. At IESE Cities in Motion, we have defined a framework for analyzing the main levers of change to help understand how they interact with each other in the different dimensions of our model, as shown in Figure 9.

Figure 9. Smart urban management model

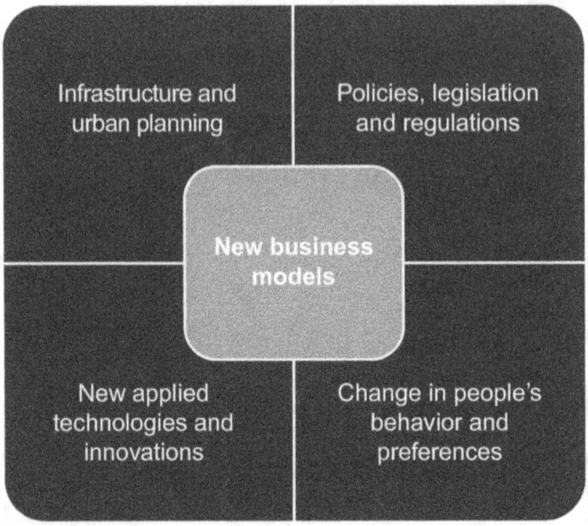

Source: Own elaboration

In the case of mobility and transportation, these key forces are playing a critical role when delivering efficient and sustainable urban mobility solutions. As previously mentioned, **new applied technologies, digitalization and innovation** are offering a wide range of new mobility services and multiplying the number of transport alternatives. Smartphones and mobility apps are also **changing people's behavior** by facilitating on-demand services and increasing choices regarding mobility. Moreover, today consumers are more concerned about the environmental impact of their decisions, showing a **change in preferences.** Similarly, **urban policies and regulations** can also be very influential by creating incentives for public transport and/or alternative modes of transportation and determining the future of automobile usage. Lastly, **infrastructures, urban planning and urban forms** are also key in shaping the mobility system of a city, since the way cities are designed - e.g. compacted cities or sprawling cities - helps to determine what kind of transport is going to be used.[6]

---

[6] This issue is going to be analyzed in more detail in the book volume *Cities and Urban Planning.*

This section analyzes some examples of international best practices and case studies to promote sustainable urban mobility. The different best practices are organized under four main broad themes: people mobility (3.1); transport demand management (3.2); urban freight and city logistics (3.3); and green mobility (3.4). Lastly, a short point on additional potential mobility solutions for the future is also discussed (3.5). For each solution, the leverages of change that play more relevant roles for that particular best practice will be highlighted.

***

3.1 People Mobility

As mentioned in the introduction, **city managers in charge of designing mobility systems in cities need to adapt to two important megatrends in regards to people mobility: a rising demand for urban mobility and a change in consumer travel habits and preferences**. As a result, cities need to develop innovative and sustainable ways to respond to these demands. They need to provide more and more flexible mobility options, minimizing congestion, improving efficiency, reducing emissions, cutting travel times, and increasing safety. All of these efforts should be aimed at improving the quality of life of the people moving around in cities.

3.1.1 Walking and Cycling

Walking and cycling are the greenest and cleanest forms of mobility. Although not suitable for long distances, walking and cycling are two of the most efficient forms of transport for short and medium distances. Additionally, they have multiple benefits for the quality of life of citizens, such as improving health, reducing GHG emissions and air and noise pollution, and lessening traffic congestion.

A good policy for sustainable urban mobility that city councils might implement is to provide additional cycling infrastructure (e.g. bike lanes, bike parking and bike hiring schemes) and/or to create pedestrian-friendly spaces (e.g. car-free zones) in order to promote both walking and cycling. Some cities around the world, such as London, Copenhagen, New York, Singapore and Paris, have already implemented pedestrian zones in some parts of their city centers. And many other urban hubs are increasing and improving their current cycle infrastructures.

Car-free zone or pedestrian zone

Photo: Pixabay, CC0.

Although these policies are mainly related to urban planning – and will be further analyzed in the book volume on this topic - the physical shape of cities and their mobility infrastructures will also influence citizens' behavior. For instance, providing more bike lanes will persuade people to invest in cycling and they will, in turn, demand that local governments increase and improve the city's cycling infrastructure (Zenghelis and Stern, 2015). Therefore, the city's policies and regulations regarding urban infrastructures will also affect people's preferences and behaviors.

***

3.1.2 Sharing Mobility Systems

The idea of sharing things is not new and, in fact, has been used for hundreds of years. However, **a conflux of current megatrends – such as rapid urbanization, resource scarcity and technological advances and connectivity – has given rise to a resurgence of the so-called "sharing economy."** These trends, combined with a growing environmental consciousness, are altering consumers' habits. The traditional thinking about how resources can and should be offered and consumed is being challenged (Cohen and Kietzmann, 2014). Today, especially in the case of young people, sharing and renting are becoming more important than buying and owning. For instance, **about 50% of car owners today can imagine sharing their vehicle in the near future** (Freese and Schönberg, 2014).

BOX 2: Shared mobility: "mobility-on-demand" vs "shared-used mobility".

Two types of shared-mobility business models can be differentiated:

1. **"Mobility-on-demand" systems,** which refers to those systems where people lend or borrow vehicles either from enterprises or from peers. These require station points for pick-up and drop-off. Examples of these structures are bike-sharing and car-sharing schemes.

2. **"Shared-used mobility"** schemes, which refers to people using or providing mobility services. These models comprise ride-sharing schemes such as car-pooling, e-hailing and taxi services or shared parking systems.

Within the sharing economy field, mobility is probably the segment that has experienced the most profound impact and penetration. This is the result of profitable opportunities offered by digitalization to personal mobility services. New technology breakthroughs, smartphones and the internet are enabling the creation and spread of new, agile business models for managing and connecting fleets and customers, allowing on-demand reservation of the specific type of vehicle people need when they need it. Car and bike-sharing schemes, for instance, have benefited greatly from real-time information on vehicles or bike availability.

Some of the main benefits brought about by shared mobility are: congestion mitigation; decrease of GHG emissions and air and noise pollution; and user benefits such as convenience, comfort and accessibility. Additionally, sharing mobility services can also complement public transit by addressing the first/last mile problem.

As a result of all these benefits and opportunities, the shared mobility sector has become one of the fastest-growing segments of the shared economy. According to a report by Roland Berger, **the global shared mobility market could reach annual growth rates between 20% and 35% from 2013 to 2020** (Freese and Schönberg, 2014).[7, 8]

a. Bike-sharing

Bike-sharing systems, bike-share schemes or smart bikes are short-term urban bicycle rental systems that allow people to pick up a bike from any self-serve bicycle station and return it to any other bicycle station point, easing point-to-point trips.

The first urban bike-share programs started in Europe in the 1960s, but their growth was relatively modest back then and they didn't really spread to cities around the world until the last generation of bike-sharing systems (ITDP, 2013).

---

[7] The report covers four sectors within the mobility market: car-sharing, ride-sharing, bike-sharing and shared-parking. The annual growth rates vary between 20% and 35%, depending on the sector.

[8] Although it is true that growth in shared-used mobility has been higher in more mature urban mobility systems, such as in Western Europe, North America and some Asian cities, several cities in emerging countries are also showing promising advances, with an increasing number of bicycles and cars being shared in their cities every year.

The most recent generation of bike-sharing systems are one of the best examples for smart urban problem-solving: it takes a familiar mode of transportation, the bicycle, and combines it with the use of new applied technology, such as smart cards, automatic docks and pick-up and drop-off stations, smart phones and real-time information (bike availability information, number of bicycles in use, empty/full stations, etc.). The use of information technology is key for the efficient and effective operation of the system, especially for the use of dock stations and for tracking and managing fluctuating demand.

Paris' Velib: bikes in dock stations

Photo: Wikimedia Commons, CCO.

The first large-scale launch of this last generation of smart bike-sharing systems was the *Velib* program in Paris in 2007. Since then, and in less than 20 years, bike-sharing schemes have multiplied in cities around the world (Figure 10). **As of the end of 2015, about 980 cities around the globe had a bike-sharing system, operating a fleet of more than 1 million bicycles** – with more and more programs launching every year (MetroBike LLC, 2015).[9]

---

[9] Interactive map on The Bike-sharing World Map, available at: <www.bikesharingmap.com>.

Figure 10: Growth of bike-sharing systems in cities around the world

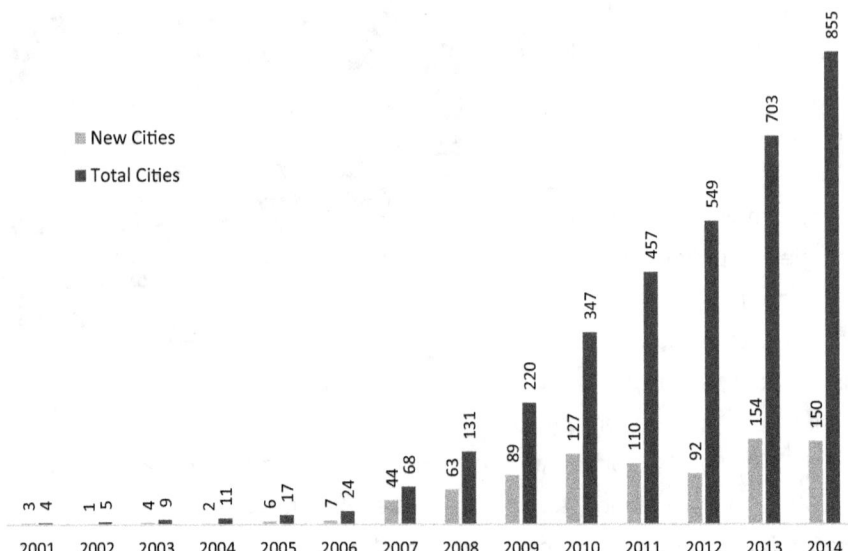

Source: Prepared by the authors based on Meddin (2014)

Bike-sharing schemes exist in different business forms and business models. They can be completely public or completely private, but in most cases they involve some form of public-private partnership. They are usually part of intermodal transport, complementing the existing public transportation system. In order to allow for a better integration with other modes of public transit, they are usually situated near public transit hubs to provide optimal service during peaks of demand.

By continent or region, Europe has the highest number of programs (60-65% of the world's total), followed by Asia (some 25%), North America and South America (each with less than 10% of the total) (Christensen, 2013). By country, as of April 2015, China led the world with more than 250 programs and an 860,000-bike fleet. Italy followed, with more than 135 programs and a fleet of approximately 15,000 bikes; next was Spain, with some 127 programs and around 27,600 bikes (Earth Policy Institute, 2015). By size of program (i.e. number of bicycles), China has leading global bike-share statistics, with all but five of the 20 largest bike-sharing programs on the planet, with cities such as Wuhan and Hangzhou at the forefront. The exceptions are Paris *Velib*, London *Santander Cycles*, Barcelona *Bicing*, New York *CitiBike* and Montreal *BIXI* (Earth Policy Institute, 2013). (Figure 11.)

Figure 11: Largest bike-sharing programs worldwide, August 2013

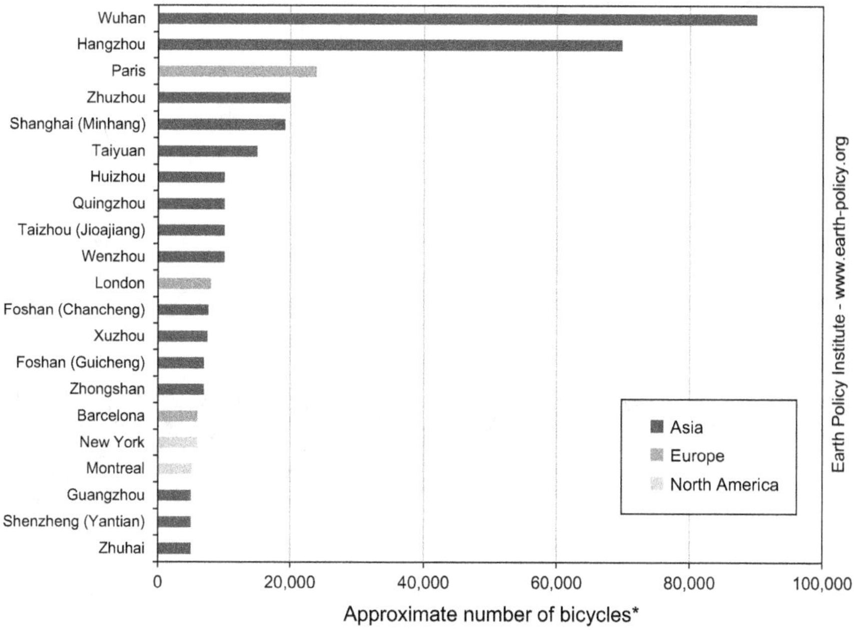

* The number of bicycles and programs changes rapidly and detailed year-to-year information is not always readily available. These numbers are for advanced, public short-duration bike-sharing programs and do not include traditional rental schemes.

The success of smart bike-sharing systems results from the fact that they are a more efficient, convenient, flexible, economic and sustainable alternative than motorized travel, especially for short-distance trips. They help diminish traffic congestion, reduce noise and pollution, improve air quality, encourage exercise and healthier habits for the citizens and increase mobility choices by providing cheap transport. However, bike-sharing systems involve challenges, such as topography and climate of the city, issues of helmet use and safety, as well as theft and vandalism (Midgley, 2011).

Despite these challenges, and in terms of revenue, the **bike-sharing market is expected to reach between €3.6 and €5.3 billion, with 20% projected annual growth by 2020** (Freese and Schönberg, 2014). These numbers exhibit the big opportunities offered by bike-sharing systems in the upcoming years. More precisely, the development of e-bikes is projected to be one of the main drivers of the bike-sharing market in the years to come.

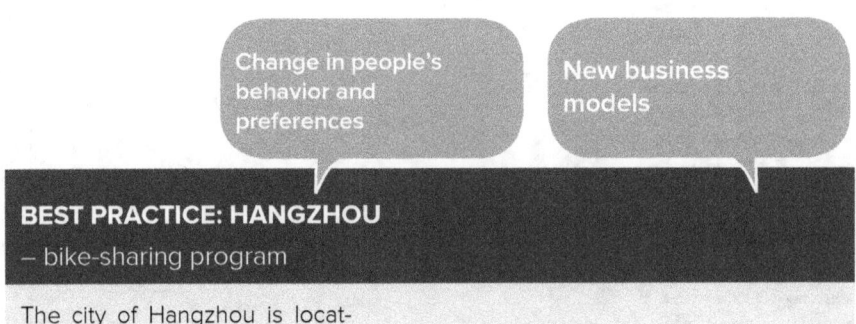

Change in people's behavior and preferences

New business models

BEST PRACTICE: HANGZHOU
— bike-sharing program

The city of Hangzhou is located in Southeast Asia, along the coast of China, 180 km. west of Shanghai. It is the capital of Zhejiang Province and the center of politics, economy, science, education and culture of the region. The city has 8 million inhabitants and the total area of the city covers 16,596 km². In economic terms, Hangzhou is one of the most prosperous cities in mainland China, with a variety of manufacturing industries, including machinery, textiles and IT. In 2013, the city's GDP rose to 834 billion yuan

Hangzhou, China

Source: Pixabay, CC0.

(US$ 137 billion), ranking first in Zhejiang Province. It boasts a GDP per capita of some $US 5,000 (similar to the level of Beijing and Shanghai).

Context

- Like other large cities in China, Hangzhou has experienced rapid economic growth and increasing urbanization rates over the past 20 years.

- Historically, China has been a country well-known for cycling. However, as the economy grew and incomes rose, people began buying more private automobiles and the country experienced a steady decline in bicycle use.

- In the Hangzhou region in particular, the proportion of personal trips made by bike dropped from 60.8% in 1997 to 33.5% in 2007 (S. A. Shaheen, Zhang, Martin, and Guzman, 2011). At the same time, the number of motorization vehicles jumped from 396,000 in 2000 to 2.14 million by the end of 2011 (Lane, Zeng, Dhingra, and Carrigan, 2015).

- This shift to car culture has made mobility in the city very complicated, with rising traffic congestion and CO_2 emissions.

Actions

- As car usage grew, Hangzhou managers realized that building additional roads wasn't the solution. They had to start looking for alternative modes of transportation that were more sustainable with the environment, which could reduce the negative automobile-related effects of mobility and that could solve the first/last mile problem at the same time.

- As part of these initiatives, on May 2008, the *Hangzhou Public Transport Corporation,* a state-owned enterprise, launched the "Hangzhou bike-sharing program." This is an example of a "government-led" model, where the Hangzhou government invested 180 million yuan Renminbi and also provided 270 million RMB discount government loans.

- As of August 2013, the program operated with approximately 69,000 bicycles and over 2,700 fixed stations (Earth Policy Institute, 2013). The bike serving spots serve from 06.00am to 08.00pm.

- The system uses smart cards, automated check-in and check-out, and dock stations. The smart cards require an initial 200 yuan ($30) deposit and users can ride the bikes for free the first hour and each subsequent hour has a cost.

- The operator tries to combine it with the public transit system and promote the "Bus and Ride" (B+R) trips, offering a discount (you get an additional 30 minutes for free if you transfer from public transit).

- In 2011, the average daily usages were about 240,000 trips with peaks of 320,000.

Outcomes

- Hangzhou has implemented a generally successful bike-sharing system. As of 2013, Hangzhou's bike-sharing program is the second largest bike-sharing program in the world, after another Chinese city, Wuhan.

Hangzhou bike-sharing station

- The system currently has some 65,000 bikes and over 2,000 stations and had to expand several times to meet the demand (Lane, et al., 2015). It is expected grow to 175,000 bicycles by 2020.

Source: Wikimedia Commons, Flickr/Payton Chung.

- In a March 2011 survey, it was found that the bike-sharing system was attracting users that simultaneously used other transport modes, such as buses, walking, autos, and taxis. In addition, around 30% of the members had incorporated bike-sharing into their everyday commute. Another 70% of the travelers use it in their commuting occasionally (S. A. Shaheen, et al., 2011).

- The survey also found out that the service was attractive to both car owners (22%) and non-members (11%). The bike-sharing program is thus facilitating new forms of travel behavior among residents.

- Automobile-related emissions have decreased as a result of the increase in bike-sharing use.

- More than 80% of bike-sharing members are satisfied with the system. The system had the highest satisfaction rate among all the city development projects.

- The Hangzhou bike-sharing program has one of the lowest theft and vandalism rates of all bike-sharing programs.
- The program provides a good example of a bike-sharing program in an emerging country, and one that is bigger than those in Europe and the Americas. However, despite being quite successful, the system needs to provide more real-time information regarding bike and parking availability, and extending hours of operation.

***

b. Car-sharing

Many urban mobility strategies of municipalities and urban planners today aim to reduce the use of private vehicles in order to reduce emissions and create more livable cities. This objective can be achieved by enhancing walking and cycling, as discussed, and by increasing use of public transport, as we will address later. However, another approach is to try to find new ways to make car use more sustainable and efficient, such as through car-sharing and ride-sharing systems. In fact, **car-sharing schemes are estimated to take approximately 5 to 11 vehicles off the road** (Navigant Research, 2013).

It is important to mention that although the ultimate goal of both car-sharing and ride-sharing systems is the same (i.e. reduce traffic congestion and its transport-related CO_2 emissions, while saving money), they are not the same. **Car-sharing refers to the joint ownership of a car or fleet of cars by the users; while ride-sharing is simply people allowing passengers to use the empty car seats in their automobile, which are owned privately**. The key difference is that the former exploits cars bought precisely for and by the car-sharing group, while the latter exploits cars already owned by people (P2P Foundation, 2015).

Car-sharing

Car-sharing is one of the major trends for the future of mobility. Similar to bike-sharing systems, car-sharing services are a model of car rental, based on membership, where people rent cars for short periods of time, often by the hour, with different stations throughout the city. **The system is attractive to customers who make only occasional use of a vehicle and a good solution to increase vehicle utilization rates, that are currently below 10%** (Zhang, 2014). In fact, a car owner spends only some 50 minutes per day in the car, whereas the rest of the day the car is parked (Cornet, et al., 2012). This means that **cars sit unused 90% of the time or more, which is highly inefficient**. Car-sharing systems and other similar services can significantly improve this situation.

Car-sharing parking space in Berkeley (US)

Photo: Wikimedia Commons

Moreover, car-sharing schemes also promote sustainable urban land use, because fewer cars need less parking space. They also contribute to reducing transport-related per capita CO_2 emissions. A study by Frost & Sullivan (2010) showed that car-sharing systems in North America – the leading world's region in per capita CO_2 emissions – diminished global carbon dioxide emissions by 482,170 fewer tons in 2009.

Since the emergence of the first car-sharing schemes in the mid-1900s in Europe, the car-sharing market has grown vastly. **As of 2014, there were over 4.8 million members sharing more than 104,000 vehicles worldwide** (S. Shaheen, 2015; Figure 12). Although Europe and North America currently account for the vast majority of car-sharing memberships and fleets, with some 40% and 35% of worldwide car-sharing schemes respectively, car-sharing is quietly showing up in several cities in emerging countries, reaching some 20% of global car-sharing members in 2014 (with almost all of them in Asia) (Lane, et al., 2015; S. Shaheen, 2015).

Figure 12: Growth of worldwide car-sharing (number of members and vehicles)

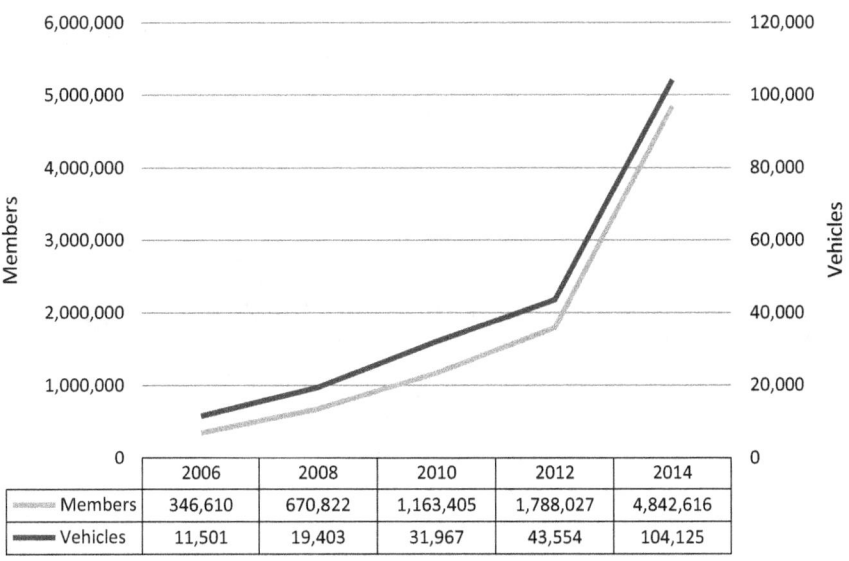

	2006	2008	2010	2012	2014
Members	346,610	670,822	1,163,405	1,788,027	4,842,616
Vehicles	11,501	19,403	31,967	43,554	104,125

Source: Prepared by the authors based on Shaheen (2015)

The number of car-sharing users is projected to grow to some 15-20 million members by 2020, depending on estimates (Lane, et al., 2015; Leveque and Moosa, 2013; Navigant Research, 2013). In terms of revenues, some studies foresee a revenue forecast of some €4–6 billion by 2020 for the car-sharing sector (Freese and Schönberg, 2014; Navigant Research, 2013); and **a market growth projection of the car-sharing sector of 23% between 2013 and 2025** (Hawksworth and Vaughan, 2014).

Car-sharing systems give travelers convenient and affordable access to a range of vehicles that are underutilized through different business models with multiple agents involved. The car-sharing market has grown from informal small firms and young startups to major multinationals, consolidated car rental agencies and leading automotive manufacturers. The market also includes cooperatives and *ad hoc* grouping, as well as public institutions, municipalities and public transport agencies. Estimates suggest that there are more than 600 different car-sharing providers around the world (Cohen and Kietzmann, 2014). These business models can be divided into the following categories: peer-to-peer (P2P), business-to-consumer (B2C), non-for-profit or cooperative schemes and public initiatives (Box 3).

BOX 3: Car-sharing business models

Type of system	Definition	Examples
Peer-to-peer (P2P)	A fleet of cars is owned by a community. The marketplace uses web and/or mobile technologies to connect and match owners of cars that are available to other potential drivers to rent.	RelayRides, Whipcar, Wheelz, Getaround, Rent'n'roll, Flight Car, Darenta
Business-to-consumer (B2C)	A company owns a fleet of cars, which are supplied at key points throughout the city, and facilitates the sharing amongst member. Members usually use their smartphones to geolocate the closest available car and B2C car-sharing firms cooperate with city governments in order to obtain preferential parking spaces (Cohen and Kietzmann, 2014).	Zipcar, StattAuto, GoGet, Car2Go and also manufacturers (such as BMW) and rental brands (such as Hertz)

Non-for-profit and Cooperatives	A local organization or community that facilitates car sharing with the goal of changing driving habits over making a profit. The members collectively contribute resources and manage the car-sharing organization.	City Car Share (San Francisco), Mobility Car Sharing (Switzerland), I-Go Carsharing (Chicago), Modo (Vancouver)
Public initiatives	Publicly-owned schemes.	Autolib' (Paris)

Source: Prepared by the authors

New business models

New applied technologies and innovations

Change in people's behavior and preferences

BEST PRACTICE: PARIS
— Autolib', the full electric car-sharing service

Paris is the capital of France, as well as the country's largest and wealthiest city. Situated on the Seine River, the City of Paris encompasses an area of some 105 km² and has a population of around 2,200,000 inhabitants (2014). The metropolitan area, the Paris Region, covers 12,012 km² and is home to more than 12 million people (2014), making it the second largest urban region in Europe after London. Known throughout the world as the "City of Light," Paris is the historical, cultural, artistic, political, commercial and economic center of France. The Paris Region is one of the wealthiest regions in Europe,

Paris, France

Source: Pixabay, CC0.

with a GDP of some US$ 700 billion and an average income per capita of US$ 28,274 in 2012 (World Cities Culture Forum, 2016).

Context

- As with other big cities, Paris' population growth and high population density required additional and more effective transportation options in order to avoid the deterioration of the city's quality of life and worsening social divisions. Gentrification of the city center has pushed all but the wealthiest out of the heart of Paris. Therefore, upgrading the existing transport network was very much needed in order to enhance accessibility.

Paris' Autolib' car-sharing services.

Photo: Ana Isabel Duch.

- After the successful Velib' bike-sharing program, Paris' city managers wanted to move forward with a new scheme that would make the city cleaner, more pleasant and less polluted.

Actions

- A commission group was created in December 2011 to create Autolib', the first public electric vehicle (EV) car sharing scheme in a large European metropolis. The Bollore group, which invested €1.7 billion in the project, teamed up with the mayor of Paris to launch the venture. Bollore operates Autolib' as part of a public service delegation contract.

- The service, which is unique in terms of size and use, allows users to rent an electric car from one of the stations located in Paris and 46 surrounding municipalities in the *Ile-de-France*.

- The program started with 66 vehicles (Bluecars) and 33 stations in October 2011. In December 2011, the system entered full service with an initial fleet of 250 Bluecars and 250 Autolib' rental stations, serving Paris and its 45 surrounding communities with a service available 24 hours a day (Dotter, 2015).

- Similar to the Velib' bike-sharing program, Autolib' is a one-way personal (individual and family) car-sharing system with technical support staff. The annual subscription is 120€ plus a rental price that varies depending on your rental package. There are also monthly, weekly and daily subscriptions.

Outcomes

- As of July 2014, the program had already grown to more than 2,500 Bluecars, 873 stations, nearly 5,000 charging terminals and parking spaces, and more than 155,000 registered subscribers (Autolib, 2015; Dotter, 2015).

Autolib' parking space in Paris.

Photo: Ana Isabel Duch.

- In 2015, the 3,000 Bluecars in operation had led to an estimated reduction of 22,500 private vehicles. This is equivalent to 164,500,000 km. driven per year by combustion engine vehicles (Autolib, 2015).

- Autolib' has therefore helped to reduce pollution and considerably reduce traffic, improving Parisians' quality of life.

- It is expected that the program will be profitable by the end of 2015. This is only four years after its launch.

- Since the beginning of its operations, Autolib' has expanded to the French cities of Lyon and Bordeaux, and the company is now targeting other markets, such as the United States and the United Kingdom.

- Despite some small problems with vandalism, in general terms the Autolib' electric car-sharing scheme has been a success.

***

c. Ride-sharing and Ride-hailing

On the one hand, ride-sharing systems (also known as carpooling, lift-sharing, ride-shares or *covoiturage*) refer to sharing rides among two or more travelers in one car, privately owned by the driver, which is headed to the same or similar destinations. **Ride-sharing or carpooling schemes involve different degrees of formality and regularity, and are mostly based on trust in the community and the platform used.**

Ride-sharing or carpooling schemes initiated in the mid-1970s and have a higher penetration in Europe and the US, where hundreds of thousands of people use them every day. When the systems first began, people usually used physical message boards to coordinate rides beforehand, agreeing when and where to meet and how to share the costs. However, with the disruption of Internet connectivity and modern mobile technologies, the spread of P2P ride-sharing schemes have been exponential. Now, most of these structures use information technologies for matching and booking, facilitating the rider to connect with the driver through Internet sites such as carpooling.com or through mobile apps like BlaBlaCar. (See Box 4.)

In general terms, carpooling schemes are not associated with drivers seeking to profit. Instead, they are aimed at supporting the car owner's vehicle costs (Cohen and Kietzmann, 2014). However, some private drivers in many of these systems also use them to earn extra money for the service beyond pure cost sharing. The main aim of ride-sharing schemes is to decrease vehicle costs (to save travelers' money); to diminish traffic congestion; and to lessen automobile GHG emissions. City managers can promote carpooling through dedicated infrastructure, such as reserved parking for car-poolers, high-occupancy vehicle (HOV) lanes and integrating the schemes with public transport.

On the other hand, **ride-hailing or e-hailing** refers to "a person who hails a car and is immediately picked up and driven to their destination for a time and distance-based fee" (Papernick, 2015). The main difference with ride-sharing is that ride-sharing involves some planning and ride-hailing is more of an on-demand immediate service.

New business models

BOX 4: **Some ride-sharing and taxi-hailing apps**

Ride-sharing	Main characteristics	Taxi-hailing app	Main characteristics
BlaBlaCar	HQ: Paris, France As of January 2016, the company was present in 22 countries with some 25 million members.	Hailo	HQ: London, UK Available in 20 cities the firm has raised over $80 million in funding and states annual sales of more than $100 million.
Carpooling.com	HQ: Munich, Germany In 2014, the firm was present in 9 countries with 6 million registered members.	GetTaxi	HQ: Tel Aviv, Israel It operates in 24 cities in 4 different countries with some 10 million users.
Carma	HQ: Cork, Ireland Founded in 2007 the start-up has secured some $10 million in funding.	MyTaxi	HQ: Hamburg, Germany It is available in 40 cities around the world and claims some 10 million users.
Djump	HQ: Chaumont-Gistoux, Belgium Available in Brussels and Paris, connect users with drivers.	EasyTaxi	HQ: Rio de Janeiro, Brazil As of 2016, it was available in 30 countries and 420 cities and had become a pioneer in online taxi services in Latin America.

Source: Author's own based on Li (2014) and other sources.

Here, Internet and mobile technologies have also played a key role, since ride-hailing schemes use different mobile apps that allow the rider to connect with the driver and order a car or a taxi via the on-demand app. The app makes use of mobile geolocation to facilitate and connect real-time ride-sharing among network members and also handles payment to the driver. Popular ride-hailing examples are the mobile apps of Lyft, China's Didi Dache and Uber (Box 5). They also include taxi-hailing apps, such as EasyTaxi and Hailo (Box 4). The ubiquity of smartphones in developed countries and their rapid spread in developing and emerging countries have enabled these companies and apps to grow at an impressive rate. For instance, in China some 170 million people are estimated to use a form of e-hailing services. Chinese scheme Didi Dache alone has more than 100 million users in 300 cities and has raised more than $800 million in venture-capital investment (Bouton, et al., 2015).

New business models

Change in people's behavior and preferences

BOX 5: Uber, a threat for taxis?

Uber, founded in the US in 2009, is probably the most famous smartphone-enabled car service app and a clear example of successful peer-to-peer ride-sharing/ride-hailing business model. The app allows the traveler to choose between different types of cars and shows him or her the waiting time of the car's arrival, the driver's profile and customer's evaluation. The company acts only as a mediator or matching service provider and it keeps 20% of the journey price.

As of 2015, Uber was present in more than 300 cities in more than 50 countries around the world, receiving over 1 million inquiries per week. In 2013, Uber had 550 employees, generating revenues of nearly €160 million (Freese and Schönberg, 2014). In 2015, the company was already valued at more than $40 billion and these numbers are expected to grow in the following years (Johnston, 2014).

However, the company is also facing some opposition, especially in European countries, where local governments and taxi drivers' associations cite regulatory concerns. The question is: will this model of ride sharing system succeed?

U B E R

All of the abovementioned websites and ride-sharing, ride-hailing and taxi-hailing apps are clear examples of how new technologies and increased connectivity are changing and shaping the mobility patterns of citizens of today, as well as creating new marketplaces for entrepreneurs.

Some studies project **revenues for the ride-sharing sector of some €3.5 to €5.2 billion for 2020 and a projected market growth of 35% per year** (Freese and Schönberg, 2014). However, the future of ride-sharing, carpooling and e-hailing schemes remains uncertain. Ride-sharing and e-hailing firms are currently in no-man's land in terms of legislation and the future of their business models will be determined by the evolution of laws affecting the sector.

***

3.1.3 Local Public Transport

As urbanization accelerates, city councils around the world need to invest in public transport as a way to improve mobility in urban areas. In fact, **a high-quality, modern, reliable and energy-efficient public transport system, that is well integrated with other modes of transport and accessible to all, is key to overcoming many of the most important challenges of urban mobility**.

The use of public transport, or mass transit, decreases the number of automobiles on the street. This reduces congestion and air and noise pollution, leads to lower GHG and CO_2 emissions, consumes less energy, saves time and fuel wasted looking for parking, uses less public space and collectively is safer than car use, since it curtails the number of car accidents.

In recent decades, some cities have increased investments in public transit systems, including Bus Rapid Transit (BRT) and rail systems, reflecting a shift from previous trends of investing in road infrastructures (Rode, et al., 2014). **Innovative urban transport systems, such as BRT, offer an effective solution for developing and emerging countries, due to significant cost savings as compared with metro or light rail systems.** Conventional bus systems have been modified to include innovative digital technologies, transforming these into high-capacity urban transport systems.

BRT systems have been proven to significantly reduce congestion-related costs in numerous developing cities such as Bogota, Lagos, Guangzhou and Johannesburg (Rode, et al., 2014). On a global level, 11 registered BRT projects in Mexico, Colombia, China, India and South Africa are forecast to reduce emissions by 31.4 million tons of CO_2 equivalent over 20 years, which equals the annual GHG emissions of more than 6.5 million cars (Fang, 2014).

Infrastructure and urban planning

BOX 6: CURITIBA, the first city implementing a bus rapid scheme

Curitiba is the 8th most populated city in Brazil, with 1.86 million habitants (3.17 million in the metropolitan area) and a GDP per capita of US $11,208.

Some 30 years ago Curitiba's forward-thinking and conscious planners anticipated the exponential growth that the city was about to experience and developed a Master Plan with the aim of integrating public transport into all other elements of the urban planning system, including land use planning (Goodman, Laube, and Schwenk, 2007). In 1974, they developed the first Bus Rapid Transit System and planned a city that would grow along designated corridors in a linear form. The downtown city would no longer be the main destination of travel, but a hub and finishing point.

Linha Verde BRT System Curitiba

Photo: Mario Roberto Duran Ortiz, CC BY-SA 3.0, via Wikimedia Commons.

Outcomes

Today Curitiba's BRT system has seven bus priority corridors consisting of 84 kilometers and benefiting 561,000 passengers every day (BRT Data, 2016). Moreover, 46% of total trips are made by public transport. This has allowed the city to reduce traffic congestion and improve air quality. According to a 1991 traveler survey, the BRT system had led to 27 million fewer car trips per year, saving about 27 million liters of fuel annually (Goodman, et al., 2007). Moreover, the buses run frequently, reliably and the stations are convenient, well-designed, comfortable and attractive. Consequently, Curitiba's Bus System has become a model for Rapid Transit, especially for developing countries.

Infrastructure and urban planning

New applied technologies and innovations

BEST PRACTICE: JOHANNESBURG
– BRT System

Johannesburg is the largest city in South Africa and the provincial capital of the Gauteng region, the wealthiest province in South Africa. The city covers an area of 1,644.96 km². In 2011, the population of the metropolitan area was 4,434,827 inhabitants (957,441 in the city), with a population density of 2,696 persons/km² (metro) (Statistics South Africa, 2011). Moreover, the city is a major economic hub. In 2008, its estimated GDP was $110 billion (at PPP) and a GDP per capita of $31,977 (Hawksworth, Hoehn, and Tiwari, 2009).

Johannesburg, South Africa

Source: Pixabay, CC0.

Context

- Africa is the continent with the poorest public transport in the world.

- Despite being a major economic hub, Johannesburg is also one of the most unequal cities in the world, with a GINI coefficient of 0.75 in 2005. Moreover, the regions and population distribution of the Johannesburg metropolitan area is a legacy of the apartheid era. Therefore, accessibility for all the different areas is very important for the city of Johannesburg.

- Daily movements account for approximately 3.5 million trips. In 2002 some 47% of those trips were made by public transport (excluding non-motorized transport). Traditionally, passenger transport has been provided by the minibus-taxi sector (more than 70%).

- The 2010 FIFA World Cup stimulated an intense interest in improving the transport system.

Actions

- With the impulse of the World Cup, three South African cities (Johannesburg, Cape Town and Port Elizabeth) initiated BRT lines. In 2009, the city of Johannesburg created the Rea Vaya Bus Rapid Transit (BRT) System with the aim to establish a safe, secure public transport system that offers efficient, reliable and frequent bus services at an affordable price.

- Other key objectives of the Rea Vaya BRT: economic growth, poverty alleviation, restructuring the apartheid city, sustainable development, and good governance.

- Main obstacle: resistance to change. In the developing world, transport in cities is usually carried out by informal transport providers (minibuses and the various types of taxi services), and in Johannesburg these providers opposed the implementation of the new BRT service.

- The Rea Vaya systems consists of three service types: trunk lines, complementary routes and feeder routes. The system has made use of ITS applications, such as AVM including GPS, Real-Time Passenger Information (RTPI) provided at bus stations, Traffic Signal Priority, CCTV at stations and on vehicles, and scheduling systems and interface with the AVLC, in order to make the system convenient and efficient (World Bank, 2011).

- Rea Vaya uses a paper ticket system for fare collection.

- Today, Johannesburg public transport consists of the following: Commuter Rail services, Urban Bus services, Minibus taxi services, Rea Vaya Bus Rapid Transit (BRT) and Express Urban rail (Gautrain).

Outcomes

- The system has been a breakthrough for Johannesburg and Africa in general. According to Rea Vaya's official webpage, as of May 2015, there were 48 stations and 10 median key stations, operational on 59 km. of trunk routes.

Rea Vaya stop in Johannesburg

Source: Flickr/Jeppestown.

- Between 40,000-60,000 passengers per day use Rea Vaya buses.

- The economic returns of the BRT system in the first phase are estimated to be close to $900 million (Zenghelis and Stern, 2015).

- Specific economic outcomes from phase 1A in 2012 include US$ 331 million in travel time savings, US$ 170 million in operating cost savings and US$ 268 million in improved road safety (Rode, et al., 2014).

- Environmental benefits: reduced road congestion, energy consumption and vehicle emissions. It is estimated that the system has reduced greenhouse gas emissions in the city by about 40,000 tons a year.

- Social benefits: the system was designed to promote social inclusion (accessible to all, including with mobility impairment); it has created employment, helped contain urban sprawl and promoted densification.

- While the system sought to benefit lower-income passengers, promote social inclusion and reduce inequalities, results show that the majority of the Rea Vaya users are mid-income dwellers (Vaz and Venter, 2012).

- The long-term plan calls for Rea Vaya routes to cover 330 km., giving more than 80% of the city's residents access to buses.

- In South Africa in general (not only in Johannesburg) there is a national commitment to ensuring that, by 2020, most residents will be no more than 500 meters away from a BRT station.

Another notable example of taking traditional technologies and using them in an innovative way is the use of cable car technology to improve mobility in informal settlements or slums. According to data provided by UN-Habitat (2010), one of every three residents live in a slum in towns and cities in developing countries. Moreover, if no policy is established to address this issue, it is estimated that the number of people living in slums worldwide might triple by 2050 (UN, 2013). Therefore, improving accessibility in informal settlements is key for achieving inclusive development in a city.

The first urban transit cable car system opened in Medellin, Colombia in 2004. It was later introduced in other emerging cities such as Rio de Janeiro (Brazil), Caracas (Venezuela) and La Paz (Bolivia).

> Infrastructure and
> urban planning

BEST PRACTICE: MEDELLIN
— improving accessibility in informal settlements

Medellin is the second largest city in Colombia and the capital of the Antioquia department. As of 2014, the city has an estimated population of 2.44 million in an area of 380.64 km². Medellin is located in the Aburra Valley and surrounded by hills. The metropolitan area houses more than 3.7 inhabitants with a population density of 6,925/km². Moreover, it is the second most important economic center of Colombia after Bogota. According to the "Global MetroMonitor" Study of the Brookings Institution, Medellin is one of the two Latin American cities with the highest growth of GDP per capita in 2014, reaching US$ 5,940. The poverty rate of Medellin's metropolitan area dropped by 22.5% during the period 2002-2008. Yet inequality remains very high (the GINI coefficient of Colombia is 0.54) and poverty levels remain worrisome.

Medellin, Colombia

Source: Pixabay, CC0.

Context

- Rapid urbanization growth in the 1960s and 1970s in Latin America resulted in inadequate low-income housing, with a high number of dwellers living in slums and informal settlements.

- In Medellin, most informal settlements are located on the city's mountainous periphery. Low-income neighborhoods are mostly situated in the north and northeast, and wealthier neighborhoods in the center and south of the city (Heinrichs and Bernet, 2014).

- Informal communities usually lack basic infrastructure and accessibility to the rest of the city is poor. Most mobility is pedestrian (citizens make more than one out of three trips on foot) or informal transport. Therefore, the segregation of these informal settlements significantly inhibits the socioeconomic mobility of the inhabitants and hinders the accessibility to jobs and education.

- Despite progress, poverty and inequality are still important issues in the city of Medellin.

Actions

- With the aim of improving accessibility in least developed suburban areas of the city and the living conditions of its residents, the city council of Medellin introduced the first mass transit cable car system for public transport, the so-called Metrocable, in 2004.

- The urban cable car was designed taking into account the city's unique hilly topography.

- The Metrocable is a public-sector project. It was designed as part of an integrated urban project of the city council (Proyecto Urbano Integrado) and managed by the local government-owned mass transit authority (EMTVA) (Heinrichs and Bernet, 2014).

- The first phase of construction entailed one cable car line, line K, that cost US\$ 24 million, covering 2 km., with a maximum of 93 cabins and a capacity of 3,000 passengers per hour in either direction (Hidalgo and Velasquez, 2015). Line K connected the municipalities of Popular and Santa Cruz (two areas with a combined population of approximately 230,000 inhabitants at that time and most of them low-income) to the metro system of other parts of the city (Heinrichs and Bernet, 2014).

- Along with the implementation of the Metrocable, other urban development projects were executed, such as the rehabilitation of surrounding public spaces, improving pedestrian infrastructure or expanding social housing (Hidalgo and Velasquez, 2015).

- The price is the same as a normal metro ticket and it can be used as a combined ticket with no extra cost. Moreover, the Metrocable operates from 4:30 a.m. to 11 p.m.

Outcomes

- The main advantage of the system is that it has helped connect low-income marginalized urban communities to the rest of the city and enhance equity between city residents.

- Moreover, it has increased access to employment for disadvantaged groups, enhanced public spaces and it is environmentally friendly (the aerial cable car system contributes little to air pollution).

Metrocable in Medellin

Source: Pixabay, CC0.

- As of 2013, the line was used by some 43,000 passengers/day with a demand near to system-capacity during peak hours.

- The time spent commuting to work by residents in some of the informal settlements before the introduction of the Metrocable was sometimes over two hours each way. Now, the travel time for those using the system has been reduced significantly.

- However, people working in the formal sector are the ones that have benefited the most from the Metrocable. For other segments of the society (housewives, children, elderly, etc.) the advantages are more limited since conventional buses and walking continue to be the main transport mode for the majority of the population in these segments of society, in both Popular and Santa Cruz (Heinrichs and Bernet, 2014).

- Due to the success of the first line K, two more lines opened: Line J covering 2.7 km. in 2008 and line L, covering 4.6 km. in 2010 (Metro Medellin, 2014). As of May 2015, these three lines of the Metrocable system were operating (K, J and L) and two more were under construction (M and H).

- Other Latin American cities with similar topography copied the system, such as Rio de Janeiro (Brazil), La Paz (Bolivia) and Caracas (Venezuela).

- Overall, the cable car system has transformed a city previously known most for its drug cartels and violence, to a one that – by expanding mobility and accessibility – has improved the quality of life of its residents and helped shape a more equitable and inclusive society.

***

3.1.4 Integrated Multi-modal Transport and Smarter Mobility Services

As mentioned above, promoting efficient and inclusive public transport is essential for achieving sustainable urban mobility. However, **effective coordination and integration among different transport options in cities is as crucial as a good public transport system**. Inter-modality or multi-modal transport refers to having access to multiple modes of transport when traveling. Multi-modal transport services facilitate trips by combining walking, bicycles, private cars, public transportation (such as buses and trains), as well as shared transportation systems.

This proliferation of transportation options brings important user benefits for citizens, such as convenience, accessibility and comfort, and allows for the shortening of commuting times. A fully integrated multi-modal transport system is needed to create a more efficient, environmentally-friendly and economical solution for cities and its metropolitan areas. Therefore, the different modes of transport not only need to be integrated, but governance policies between the local and the metropolitan authorities should be coordinated and aligned to successfully prioritize and harmonize planning.

New digital technologies can be very useful in improving and facilitating integrated multi-modal systems. For instance, smart ticketing and integrated travel information can be very helpful in making public transport user-friendly and facilitating accessibility for all citizens.

a. Smart Ticketing

Integrated ticketing across all services, operators and vehicle types that make pricing and payment more convenient is essential to make inter-modal travel an appealing option for city dwellers. Ticketing systems that are simple, transparent and easy to understand for everyone are key for a successful transport system. Advances in ICTs have made advance ticketing and the modification of ticketing for public transport faster and more convenient. Examples include contact-less payment through smart cards that allow users to travel on different modes of public transport, or park and ride services that integrate parking fees and public transport fares.

Contact-less smart cards (CSC) systems used for public transport fare payment and collection have become a key component for a fully integrated multimodal ticketing systems in many cities around the world.

CSC systems offer a cost-effective and convenient method for an easier payment for transport services across different modes. Moreover, smart payment systems can also provide service operators with valuable data on the behavior and mobility patterns of its users. Therefore, smart cards can offer considerable benefits both to the users and the operators.

New applied technologies and innovations

BEST PRACTICE: HONG KONG
– "Octopus system", a contact-less smart card

Hong Kong is a city and a Special Administrative Region of the People's Republic of China, situated in the southeast coast of China. With some 7.24 million people in an area of only 1,104 km², Hong Kong is one of the most densely populated metropolises in the world. Additionally, it is one of the world's leading financial centers and one of the wealthiest cities in the world with a GDP of $412.300 billion and a GDP per capita of $56,428 (2015 estimates).

The city of Hong Kong

Source: Pixabay, CC0.

Context

- Hong Kong is one of the most crowded cities in the world. Due to geographical urban form, the city is dominated by high-rise buildings.

- A total of 14 million person-trips per day are made on various modes of transport (Picco, 2014).

- Public transport and walking make up 92% of the city's modal split.

- Hong Kong's public transport is a high-quality, advanced, multi-modal network. It is based on rail transport, bus, minibus, tram, ferries and taxis. However, the city needed a well-integrated system to give users access to all modes with an easy, fast and convenient ticketing and fare payment system.

Actions

- In September 1997 the Octopus Card was created in order to collect fares for the public transport (PT) system. It was the second contact-less smart card system in the world.

- Five competing PT operators created a joint venture company in order to develop and operate the smart card system.

- In 2000, the system to pay PT fares was extended to a general e-payment system for small-value transactions. The Octopus card not only allows you to travel on PT but also to pay for parking, shops, fast-food outlets, phone use and other leisure facilities.

Outcomes

- Hong Kong has introduced a fast, reliable, cost-effective and convenient method with the Octopus Card. Both the number of cards and the number of transactions made with them have progressively increased over the years, which shows a high degree of traveler satisfaction and a high level of systems' penetration.

Octopus Cards

Source: Wikimedia Commons, Wuxxx790.

- Today, there are around 22 million cards in circulation and some 95% of people in Hong Kong, aged 15 to 64, use Octopus to travel, shop or eat (Picco, 2014).

- Along with a good urban planning and transport infrastructure, IT facilities such as the Octopus card have helped achieve a low rate of car ownership (73 per 1,000 citizens) and a dominant role for public transport in an overcrowded city.

***

b. Integrated Travel Information

New technologies are reshaping the game. **Transport information systems, real-time analytics and big data on traffic conditions can help travelers select the most cost-effective or time-appropriate mode of transport, avoid traffic congestions and/or optimize traffic flows**. For instance, in-vehicle connectivity through mobile phone enables many possibilities for easing mobility and reducing congestion, traffic jams and unnecessary GHG emissions. But this is just one example of a wide number of new urban mobility services that are being developed and implemented in cities around the world. In 2014, global venture-capital investments into mobility services amounted to more than $5 billion, up from less than $10 million in 2009 (Bouton, et al., 2015). All of these developments show that advances in software and information technologies will play a crucial role optimizing traffic flows and providing solutions to congestion and traffic challenges in urban areas.

Mobile Services and Smartphone apps

Smartphones are ubiquitous and some apps are changing the way people choose their mobility options and/or plan their routes. For instance, some apps and webpages have been developed in order to give information on traffic flows and/or different public transit options, offering users greater flexibility when planning a route by car; or when planning and monitoring their public transport trips or multi-modal transport, including information on various modes of transport available nearby (automobile, on-demand services, public transport, etc.), even providing pricing and time (Box 7).

BOX 7: Mobility services for route planning: the cases of Waze, Moovit and Citymapper

One example of mobility service for route planning is the Waze app. **Waze** is a mapping app that crowd-sources traffic data and gets detailed user-generated real-time data to drivers in order to avoid traffic conditions and bottlenecks. The platform connects drivers to one another, creating local driving communities to work together so as to improve traffic flows. Moreover, the app company has also partnered with a number of cities – such as Barcelona, Boston, Jakarta and Rio de Janeiro – to integrate its data into the city's intelligent-transportation system traffic-control center in order to allow the optimization of traffic flows (Bouton, Knupfer, Mihov, and Swartz, 2015).

Another app that seeks to improve flexibility of personal mobility is **Moovit**. Moovit is an Israeli- founded free app that allows travelers to plan and monitor their public transport journeys. The app makes it easier to use local public transport by providing the fastest, most comfortable way to get from point A to point B by integrating stop, route, schedule and real-time information for all transport types. As of December 2015, the app had 30 million users in 700 cities in 58 countries around the world.

Citymapper, a British start-up founded in 2008, is an integrated real-time trip planning application. It was firstly launched in London and as of June 2015 is available in 22 cities in 4 different countries. It consists of an online service and a mobile app that suggests different travel itineraries from points A to B in the selected city, using all public transit modes, bike-share programmes, walking routes, etc. The Citymapper app enables the user to choose the optimal route offering real-time service updates, together with pricing information and even estimated calorie use.

The examples in Box 7 demonstrate how transportation apps can improve urban travel experience, contribute to better traffic conditions and facilitate inter-modal transportation in cities. Mobile services and smartphones apps are becoming a successful and key tool on the frontline of digitized intermodal transport and will continue playing an important role in urban mobility in the future.

***

3.2 Transport Demand Management

Increasing connectivity and digitalization are two of the biggest megatrends of the 21st century and, as in many other different sectors, are playing a crucial role in improving the management of traffic and transport systems in cities.

Different terms are used to refer to the application of ICTs in the field of mobility and transport, such as info-mobility or intelligent transport systems (ITS). But regardless of the term use, the fundamental idea is that advances in ICTs and connectivity in the transport sector generate a high volume of data, so-called "big data," with the potential to be used as a source of transport efficiency. As a result, these large amounts of information available can improve traffic and operations, advance operations management and public transport planning, develop quality travel experience for customers by offering a better understanding of travelers, while leading to new mobility services and applications.

3.2.1 Real-time Traffic Management

The use of Intelligent Transportation Systems (ITS) applications for effective service control in cities can notably improve efficiency of the system, reduce traffic accidents, increase safety, decrease travel times and increase the usability of public transport services. This is of crucial importance both for city managers and city dwellers. From city managers' point of view, ITS applications allow city administrators to manage traffic and monitor public transport in a more effective and efficient way. ITS technology can help better coordinate and manage traffic flows via satellite-based applications, GPS (global positioning systems) and wireless data transmission. For instance, smart traffic systems in Singapore can predict traffic congestion with 90% accuracy, which significantly increases the effectiveness and efficiency of the system (Townsend, 2014). On the other hand, from the travelers' perspective, ITS can provide better and more accurate information on trip options, improve the quality of their travels, help avoid congested areas and improve parking management and availability.

New applied technologies and innovations

BEST PRACTICE: VIENNA
— traffic and travel information

Vienna is the capital and largest city of Austria, located in Western Europe. The city has a population of 1.7 million inhabitants in an area of 414.65 km² and a population density of 4,326/km². Moreover, the Austrian capital is a cultural, social and economic center with a GDP of €77,942 million (2011) and a GDP per capita of €47,200 (2013). Vienna is often considered a city with a high quality of life. For instance, the *Economist Intelligence Unit's Global Liveability Ranking* 2015 listed Vienna as the 2nd most "liveable" city and in the 2016 *Mercer Quality of Life Ranking*, Vienna earned the top spot.

Vienna, Austria

Source: Pixabay, CC0.

Context

- The metropolitan area of Vienna has some 3.5 million inhabitants (40% of all Austrians) and approximately 200,000 daily commuters.

- The amount of congestions and delays in and out the city were traditionally very high.

Actions

- In order to decrease congestions and delays, the three federal provinces of Vienna, Lower Austria and Burgenland recognized the potential of ITS and established a cooperative telematics project called *"ITS Vienna Region"* in 2006.

- To run the project, the federal provinces integrated their three public transport systems into an association called *Verkehrsverbund Ost-Region* (VOR GesmbH) or public transport association Vienna Region.

- The aim of the project was to create a regional intermodal traffic system that would offer real time traveler information services.

- Information of traffic is permanently updated for all traffic modes and the entire Vienna Region. It is free for the public and based on traffic, city development and environmental policies.

- The city also created the so-called *AnachB* site and mobile app that provides users with information on traffic situations, allowing citizens to determine the best route to a destination (by public transport, bike, car or on foot) and offering an objective comparison of travel times and CO_2 emissions between the different transportation options. The site has information for all Austria and particularly the federal provinces of Vienna, Lower Austria and Burgenland. *AnachB* uses numerous sensors and GPS-based vehicle data and is updated every seven and a half minutes.

- Also developed was a multi-modal mobility platform, the so-called SMILE project (Smart Mobility Info and Ticketing System Leading the Way for Effective E-Mobility Services). The project was jointly created by two city-owned enterprises and the Austrian Federal Railways (ÖBB). Suppliers of mobility services such as e-car sharing, e-bike sharing or parking grounds can also use the platform to provide their services (Manville et al., 2014).

ITS Vienna Region

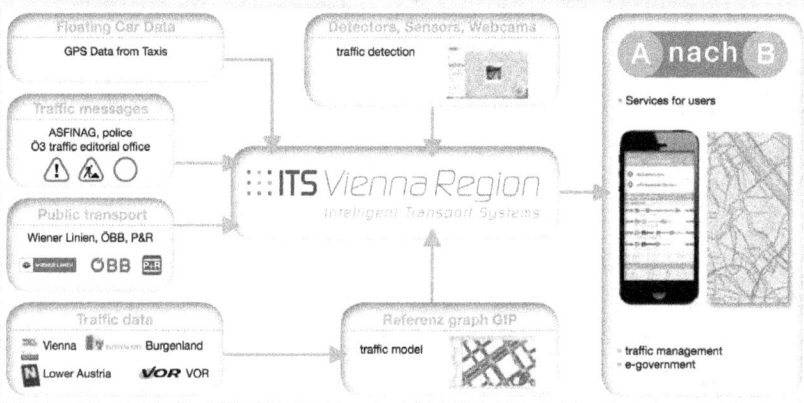

Source: AnachB at <http://www.anachb.at/>

Outcomes

- This is a good example of coordinated transport governance policies between local and metropolitan authorities.

- The project had an efficiency impact, through modal shift and better informed passengers. Additionally, it also had some important socio-economic impacts, since route guidance is free of charge and accessible for all social groups.

- The *AnachB* had positive user acceptance with 1 million requests/month (Urban ITS Expert Group, 2013).

- After three years at the development stage, preliminary results of the SMILE project were presented in May 2015. An online survey found that 75% of users were satisfied; 48% of the respondents stated that since using SMILE, they use public transport more often; and 21% reported using their private car less frequently. Additionally, combining car and public transport occurred more frequently for 26% of the pilot users. Some 20% of the respondents said they combined a bike ride with public transport more often (City of Vienna, 2015).

- Today, all transportation and urban planning initiatives are part of a greater initiative called "Smart City Wien," in which the city managers aim to make the city a major European player in smart city technologies.

***

3.2.2 Parking Management: Smart Parking

In general terms, it is always better to promote alternative modes of transportation rather than private automobile use. However, when this is not possible, parking management becomes crucial, especially in medium and large cities.

Two important facts in relation to parking need to be highlighted. First, **the vast majority of cars sit idle 90% of the time**. Second, **on average, up to 30% of cars in congested downtown traffic are actually people looking for parking**, also called "cruising" for parking (Shoup, 2006). According to some estimates, a car takes an average of 3.5 to 14 minutes each to find an open spot (Shoup, 2006). This fact results in long cruising times for individual drivers, traffic congestion, unnecessary pollution and other social and environmental costs. Therefore, finding solutions to tackle this problem should be essential for city planners around the world.

With this aim, some cities have recently implemented "smart parking programs." Smart parking refers to the application of technology and data to help manage and hopefully, improve the parking infrastructure with the ultimate goal of creating more livable and sustainable cities (Xerox, 2014). A smart parking system helps drivers find a vacant spot using sensors in each parking space that detect the presence or absence of a vehicle, directing incoming drivers to available locations. Moreover, some smart parking systems include smart meters that can vary prices by demand in order to maintain a minimum of spaces vacant (at peak hours, prices rise), and collect fees using a wide variety of payment methods.

Smart parking systems are a good example of how the application of real-time data and analytics can improve the life of citizens by reducing driving time, traffic congestion and associated air pollution and CO_2 emissions. Although only a few cities in the developed world have started using these systems, according to estimates, on-street parking spaces enabled with smart technology are expected to surpass 1 million worldwide by 2024 (Navigant Research, 2015).

BOX 8: Madrid Smartparking: managing urban mobility with innovation.

To reduce "cruising time", i.e. time spent looking for parking, a new pilot project called *Madrid Smart Parking* was tested in 2015 in Madrid, Spain. The project is the result of a public-private collaboration among some of the city's main stakeholders: the Madrid City council, Ferrovial Servicios, a Spanish infrastructure operator multinational company and a start-up company, Apparcar.

The Apparcar solution is a free app that enables drivers to search the nearest available parking space with just one click. The project was tested in Las Tablas neighborhood in Madrid with 131 parking spaces ready to be reserved. During a 3-month trial, the app was downloaded 1,700 times and 6,600 parking reservations were made through the system. The project has resulted in an estimated parking time savings of more than 600 hours.

More information on: http://www.apparcar.com.

New business models

New applied technologies and innovations

BEST PRACTICE: SAN FRANCISCO
— SF*park* as a way to improve parking.

San Francisco is the economic and cultural center of Northern California, in the United States. It covers a land area of about 121 km² and has a population of 852,469 inhabitants (2014). It is the second densest city of the USA after New York. The metropolitan area has more than 4.5 million inhabitants, and in 2013 the five-county San Francisco metropolitan area had a GDP of US$ 388.3 billion. The

San Francisco, USA

Source: Pixabay, CC0.

city is a popular tourist destination and is also the headquarters of many large companies and major banking institutions.

Context

- San Francisco, like many major cities, has a problem of traffic congestion.
- The San Francisco Municipal Transport Authority (SFMTA) plans, manages, and operates the city's transport system, including local public transit (Muni), walking, biking, roads, on-street parking, parking enforcement, and a significant portion of the city's off-street parking supply.

Actions

- With the aim to ease congestion and reduce cruising times, the city government started developing initiatives and ideas about how to direct cars to available parking spaces.
- In November 2008, the SFMTA's Board of Directors approved the legislation that implemented the SFpark project. SFpark is a federally-funded initiative focused on using new technologies and policies to improve parking in San Francisco.
- In the summer of 2010, the city launched the SFpark pilot program. SFpark uses sensor technology (smart parking meters) and wireless communication technology to collect and distribute real-time information about the number and location of available parking spaces in San Francisco.
- SFpark uses demand-responsive pricing to open up parking spaces on each block and reduce circling and double-parking in congested areas.
- Sensors are used to adjust parking rates to meet demand and encourage turnover of parking spaces. Real-time checking of parking spaces and charges help driver's decisions on his or her mode of transport.
- Drivers can access information on the site or by cell phone, and can also pay by cell phone.

Outcomes

- Over the course of the SFpark pilot project, parking rates were lower: the average hourly rate at meters was reduced by 11 cents (SFpark and SFMTA, 2014).

- Parking availability improved considerably, with a decrease in the time taken to find a parking by 43%.

- Increased payment options: Now it is easier to pay and avoid parking citations.

- Reduced pollution: GHG emissions decreased. According SF*park* pilot evaluation program, drivers generated 7 metric tons of GHG emissions per

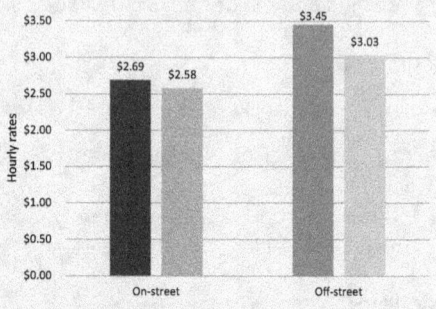

Hourly parking rates in SFpark areas

Source: SF*park* (2014).

day looking for parking in pilot areas. This dropped by 30% by 2013, compared to a decrease of 6% in control areas (SFpark and SFMTA, 2014).

- On-street parking availability improved by 22% during peak periods.

- Traffic volume decreased by approximately 8% and vehicles miles traveled also decreased by 30% from 8,134 miles per day in 2011 to 5,721 miles per day by 2013 (SFpark and SFMTA, 2014).

***

3.3 Urban Freight and City Logistics

People mobility has conventionally been the focal point of urban mobility and transport. However, cities are also centers of economic activity, i.e. places where the production, distribution and consumption of goods and services takes places. Therefore, efficient urban goods transport strategies are crucial in order to satisfy the material demands of city dwellers. This means not only an efficient distribution of material goods, but also an effective management of the waste resulted from these economic activities (See Book Volume *Cities and the Environment* (Berrone, Ricart, and Duch, 2016)).

As a city develops, economic activity increases, along with the number of goods moving within that city. Today, freight transport accounts for up to 20% of urban traffic, 30% of street occupation, some 50% of urban transport GHG emissions, 2-5% of the urban employment and 3-5% of urban land use (Savy, 2012; UN-Habitat, 2013). What is more, demand for urban goods mobility is expected to triple from 2010 to 2050 (Van-Audenhove, DeJongh and Durance, 2015). Therefore, the social and economic costs of goods movement have a direct effect on cities; and the neglect of urban freight distribution and management could become a major obstacle to sustainable urban mobility.

Some of the challenges faced by urban goods transport are the same as those of human mobility, e.g. traffic congestion, transport-related GHG emissions and safety. However, others are sector-specific, such as parking for deliveries, reserve logistics flows (waste, recycling and garbage collection) and e-commerce. There are three principal components of city logistics: the modes or means of transport for freight delivery, the infrastructures allowing freight flows and the operations related to their organization and management (UN-Habitat, 2013).

Diverse industries use trucks to meet their transport needs. The same road infrastructure used for goods transport is used for personal mobility, resulting in greater traffic congestion and accidents. Consequently, **an efficient combination of both urban passenger traffic and urban goods traffic is becoming increasingly challenging**. Improving logistic flows through effective city logistics strategies is crucial for the success of an efficient urban mobility planning and transport system of a city.

The "last mile" problem

Cities are often the final destinations of freight flows. In fact, the delivery of goods accounts for a significant share of traffic in cities. While bringing numerous economic benefits, the so-called "last mile" presents critical problems for freight distribution in urban areas such as traffic congestion, delays, additional costs, deteriorating air quality and rising carbon emissions. The last-mile problem is especially critical because it involves a range of stakeholders, such as local public authorities, transportation companies and retailers, who have different interests and objectives (Van-Audenhove, et al., 2015).

To optimally coordinate freight logistics, the last mile of urban goods transport requires a redesign of distribution strategies more suitable to an urban context. In recent years, many urban mobility strategies have been put in place by different municipalities to solve this problem, some more successful than others. Better coordination of freight delivery can save money and reduce traffic congestion and air and noise pollution. **Innovative logistics plans often require the cooperation of local authorities with logistics providers**. These plans can consist of a varied array of initiatives, such as the consolidation of goods, urban distribution centers, parking areas for delivery, delivery time windows, lorry lanes, delivery to home or park-and-ride sites.

Policies, legislation and regulations

BEST PRACTICE: NEW YORK
– Night delivery

New York City is the most populous city in the United States and one of the most important economic, financial, cultural and political centers of North America and the world. It houses around 8.5 million inhabitants in an area of 1,214 km² with an urban density of 10,756/km². NYC is a global hub of business and commerce, and the world's premier financial center. In 2012, the New York City Metropolitan Area generated a gross metropolitan product (GMP) of over US$ 1.33 trillion. Moreover, in 2013, the Metropolitan area of NY-NJ-PA had a GDP per capita of US$ 69,074.

New York, USA

Source: Pixabay, CC0.

Context

- New York, like many other big cities, has very high congestion levels, especially in peak hours.

- Urban freight delivery was contributing to the rising traffic congestion in the city.

Actions

- In 2002, the Council of Logistics Management asked the New York State Department of Transport (NYSDOT) to study solutions for urban freight delivery. Specifically, they asked for a research study on how to foster off-hour delivery (OHD) (Holguin-Veras, Wang, Browne, Hodge, and Wojtowicz, 2014). "Off-hour deliveries" are those taking place between 10 p.m. and 6 a.m.

- Night deliveries can help relieve peak daytime road congestion and therefore make better use of road infrastructure capacity. The overall goal of the project was to improve travel speeds, reduce congestion and reduce costs for business.

- In 2011, the City of New York integrated OHD into its sustainability plan. The project was piloted by the NYC Department of Transport together with Rensselaer Polytechnic Institute and funded by the US Department of Transport.

- The pilot was tested in Manhattan by 33 companies that varied in size and were divided into carriers and receivers. They switched delivery operations to the off-hours for a period of 1 month.

- A system of incentives to the receivers of deliveries was designed, combined with remote sensing monitoring, based on GPS-enabled smartphones. The financial incentive for the receiver was up to $1,000 (US Department of transportation, NYC, and Rensselaer Polytechnic Institute, 2013).

- After the pilot, the official program – called NYC deliverEASE – was launched. Almost 150 restaurants, groceries stores, retailers and other businesses participated. They received a $2,000 cash incentive.

Outcomes

- Organizations that participated in the NYC deliverEASE program include: Sysco, Whole Foods Markets, Wakefern, Gristedes Supermarkets, the Waldorf Astoria, Chefs Warehouse, The Beverage Works, CVS, New Deal Logistics, the Grand Central Partnership, the Downtown Alliance, and the Manhattan Chamber of Commerce (Mullaney, 2013).

Overnight truck delivery

Source: Flickr/IntangibleArts.

- This is a good example of public-private partnership and multi-stakeholder cooperation. However, many problems between the different actors involved appeared through the implementation of the project due to uncertainty of the level of involvement from other parts (Holguin-Veras, et al., 2014).

- The economic benefits of a full implementation of the OHD program are estimated to be between $147 and $193 million per year, corresponding to savings on travel time and environmental pollution for regular-hour traffic, as well as productivity increases for the freight industry (Holguin-Veras et al., 2012).

- On average, travel speeds from the depot to the first customer in Manhattan increased from 11.8 miles/hour in the morning peak hours (6 to 9 a.m.), to 20.2 miles/hour in the off-hours (7 p.m. to 6 a.m.) (Holguin-Veras, et al., 2012).

- The financial incentives were found to be very effective. Moreover, participants reported they were very satisfied with the system. Receivers gained more time for customer interactions during business hours, more on-time deliveries and an increased reliability of shipments (US Department of Transportation, et al., 2013).

- Travel time savings compared to regular-hour traffic were found to be substantial, amounting to 6% travel time reductions in Manhattan, or about 48 minutes per delivery tour (Holguin-Veras, et al., 2012).

- Carriers saved time and money, including fewer parking tickets, with an average monthly savings of $500 to $1,000 per truck (US Department of Transportation, et al., 2013). Moreover, they reported less stress and an increased feeling of safety.

- Important environmental pollution reductions were achieved.

- Noise impact on surrounding communities, disturbing resident's sleep, could be an important side effect of the system. Legislation requiring low-noise equipment might be considered, which could be problematic since it would require additional investment from the freight industry.

***

3.4 Green Mobility and Low Emissions Zones

Tackling climate change requires actions in a wide variety of fields and dimensions. Although this issue is further analyzed in the volume *Cities and the Environment* in this series, a special mention must be made here, due to the high level of interdependence between current mobility patterns and climate change and the environment. In fact, as a result of the predominance of oil-based fuels and motorized transport for both people's and goods' transport, the mobility and transportation sector is one of the major contributors to strain on the environment and one area where there is still much room for improvement. Therefore, **it is critical to start adopting strategies and initiatives to improve energy efficiency in the mobility sector; to start looking for alternative fuels; and to develop sustainable eco-friendly ways of mobility and transportation.**

3.4.1 Clean and Energy Efficient Vehicles

Green mobility implies the use of low-carbon and efficient vehicle technologies. These new technologies could help introduce cars that contribute toward reducing both traffic congestion and pollution on the streets. For instance, cleaner vehicles – such as hybrids and electronic vehicles (EVs) – decrease local air and noise pollution and GHG emissions, which boosts quality of life and contributes to the better health. Green mobility is gaining critical importance. For this reason, cleaner fuels and more efficient vehicles will play critical roles in the shift towards sustainable mobility.

Cleaner fuels

The use of cleaner fuels in vehicles, such as biodiesel or biogas, is seen as a key element towards energy independence from fossil fuels. Introducing cleaner vehicles and fuels can be costly and its implementation slow. However, its benefits are very important. This is why many cities around the world are introducing initiatives and implementing actions that incentivize the use of clean and energy-efficient public and private vehicles, both for passenger and freight transport. The implementation of cleaner vehicles by public institutions initiates the demand for fueling facilities. Once they are installed, cleaner vehicles can be more easily supported to individual car users. (See Box 9.).

BOX 9: Dubai, first to fuel municipal vehicles on 100% local waste cooking oil

In February 2015, the municipality of Dubai and Neutral Fuels LLC signed a ground-breaking deal to run municipal vehicles with clean biodiesel fuel (Thorpe, 2015). With this deal, the most populous city of the United Arab Emirates became the first city in the world to formally adopt biodiesel made 100% locally from 100% waste cooking oil for use in its municipal vehicles. The biodiesel fuel will cost the same as conventional diesel, but it will result in fewer carbon monoxide emissions.

This strategy is part of the UAE's vision for a sustainable future and a good example of how municipalities can implement sustainable solutions to promote clean fuels and fuel efficiency

Electric vehicles (EVs)

New technologies are reshaping urban mobility systems. In previous sections, we have seen how digitalization is changing personal mobility, easing sharing mobility systems and integrating inter-modal transportation. But two other major technological trends are also altering the game: electrification and automation. (See point 3.5 for automation.)

Electric power can significantly increase the energy efficiency of a car, while decreasing the pollutants emitted. New technologies in electrification are key in the evolution of storage and charging technologies for EVs, making them more accessible. Although short-term estimates of EVs remain still

Electric vehicle in Amsterdam

Source: Pixabay, CC0.

significantly lower than the less expensive fossil-fuel vehicles, battery costs for EVs are currently falling, prompting optimistic expectations for a higher use of EVs in the future.

According to IHS, a market-research firm, **annual sales of battery-powered EVs and hybrids will increase from about 2.3 million units in 2014 to 11.5 million by 2022, representing 11% of the global market** (Bouton, et al., 2015). Additionally, some studies estimate that **more than 500,000 EVs were sold in 2015,** a trend that is only expected to keep growing in the years to come (King, 2015).

These estimates are expected to be even higher in cities, where driving distances are shorter and the problem of running out of battery is less worrisome. In fact, several cities, mostly in Europe and North America, have introduced electric vehicles in their public transport systems (bus, tram, etc.), and even in car-sharing systems such as the *Paris' Autolib'* program (See Best Practice: Paris).

***

3.4.2 Congestion Charges and Low Emission Zones

Due to the high social cost of car-centered city designs, many local governments around the world have implemented a range of strategies and initiatives to promote the use of alternative modes of transport that seek to minimize car use. Some of these strategies, policies or regulations are: car-free zones, low-emission zones, congestion-charging schemes and/or taxes on fuel prices.

One of the strategies that has proven to be effective is congestion-charging schemes. Congestion charges or congestion pricing is a measure aimed at reducing congestion by imposing charges for entering some parts of the city, such as the city center, and/or for parking. The charges consist mainly of a toll that can also change during the day to adapt to peak hours. Some cities, such as London, Singapore or Stockholm, have used congestion charges for some years already with positive results, such as reductions in traffic congestion and GHG emissions.

Policies, legislation and regulations

BEST PRACTICE: STOCKHOLM
— Road toll collection system and electric vehicles

The City of Stockholm is the capital of Sweden and the most populous city of the country with some 900,000 inhabitants. Greater Stockholm - Stockholm County - is an area consisting of 25 municipalities with a total population of more than 2 million and an urban density of 3,597/km². Greater Stockholm is built on 14 islands woven together by 54 bridges and covering an urban area of some 381 km². The Stockholm region is the economic, political and cultural center of Sweden and one of the most important economic and financial hubs in the Nordic region. In 2011, its regional GDP per capita was 1,500 billion Swedish kronor (SEK), accounting for 42% of Sweden's GDP and placing among the top 10 regions in Europe for GDP per capita (Stockholm Business Region, 2013).

City of Stockholm

Source: Pixabay, CC0.

Context

- Stockholm was built on a harbor surrounded on all sides by lakes. This specific geographical and urban context presents a number of challenges organizing the accessibility to the city center, since most commuters had to cross very congested bridges to access it every day.

- Despite a good public transportation system and a relatively small population, the city's traffic congestion during peak hours in and out of the city center was very high, resulting in a deteriorating environmental situation, bad air quality and diminished quality of life of its dwellers.

- In 2006, prior to the implementation of congestion charges, the cordon around the inner city was crossed by 530,000 vehicles and 800,000 transit passengers each day (Tools of Change, 2014).

- Stockholm is well known for its green projects (energy, building, transport) and has an environmentally conscious population.

Actions

- With the objective of reducing congestion, increasing accessibility and improving the environment – and after some research – the City Council decided to test a congestion-charging scheme in 2006.

- The system was simple: a single-road toll collection system for vehicles going in and out of the inner city. Toll charges were based on vehicles license plates that were read by cameras using Automated Number Plate Recognition (ANPR) software.

- The *Vägverket* (Swedish Road Administration) was the body responsible for the administration of the charge, while IBM was the prime contractor responsible for solution design, development and operation.

- Tariffs varied according to time of day, with higher charges during peak periods.

- Vehicles using alternative fuels were exempt from the congestion charge.

- Funding was provided by the National Transportation Agency. The system cost roughly $215 million CAD to install (Tools of Change, 2014).

Outcomes

- After a seven-month trial, from January to July 2006, followed by a referendum, the charges were made permanent (Tools of Change, 2014).

- The system takes $10 million CAD a year to operate. Average annual revenues are about $107 million CAD, giving the system a simple payback of about two years (Tools of Change, 2014).

- An evaluation of congestion charging for the period 2006 to 2008 indicated an approximate 20% reduction of traffic in the congestion charge zone (96,000 vehicles per day), and this level of reduction has been maintained (CIVITAS, 2013; Tools of Change, 2014). Congestion was reduced by 30-50% on arterials.

- The main barriers to congestion charging were public and political opposition. However, after some initial opposition, by 2011, public support for the charging scheme reached some 70%.

- Emissions in the inner city decreased by 10-14% as a direct result of the congestion charge (Tools of Change, 2014). However, if we take into account all the different strategies put in place by the city council for reducing its carbon footprint on the planet since 1990, the Stockholm government has managed to reduce its GHG emissions by 25-30% (Van-Audenhove, et al., 2015).

Stockholm's congestion tax cordon map

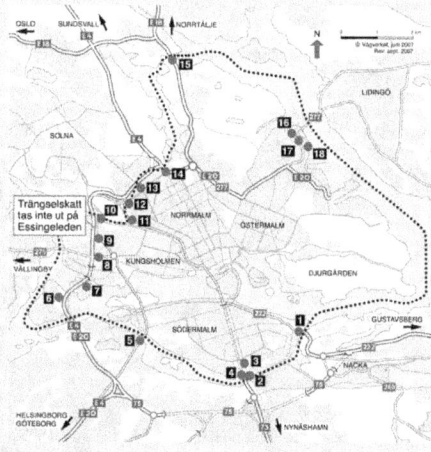

Source: Wilson (2012).

- The net social benefit of the congestion charging system is estimated to be €65 million per year (Tools of Change, 2014).

- Additional strategies have been implemented in the past few years in Stockholm to encourage a modal shift towards public transport, walking and cycling. These include a 30Km/h speed limit in residential areas; a substantial improvement of the cycling network; and, in May 2011, the Stockholm City Council adopted an EV/PHEV strategy with the goal of becoming a leading EV city, fossil-free in the inner-city by 2030 and region-wide by 2050. Stockholm's transport authorities have committed to ensuring that public transport services are using green vehicles – there are 229 methane buses, 768 ethanol buses and 224 RME-fueled buses (Van-Audenhove, et al., 2014). Moreover, the city has been testing the performance of a fleet of 50 EVs throughout Sweden, incentivizing EV owners and exempting them from vehicle tax for the first five years (OECD/IEA, 2012).

- With all these strategies, the transport-related CO_2 emissions dropped from 1,430 kg. per capita in 2011 to 1,348 kg. per capita in 2013 (Van-Audenhove, et al., 2014). Not only have CO_2 emissions been reduced, but the number of transport-related fatalities also decreased from 21 per million in 2011 to 9 per million in 2013.

- Also, an increase in the number of vehicles using alternative fuels in the Swedish capital has been observed and the number of bikers has doubled in recent years. Roughly 12% of Stockholm dwellers shifted from private motorized vehicles to public transport and cycling.

- In 2010, the European Commission named Stockholm the first European Green Capital.

- Lastly, the city has not only managed to reduce its GHG emissions and traffic congestion levels, but has also grown its economy by 41% since the 1990s (Zenghelis and Stern, 2015). This shows that being environmentally friendly and establishing ambitious environmental targets does not negatively affect economic performance.

***

3.5 Other Mobility Solutions of the Future

In the previous sections, we have analyzed some of most recent developments in the urban mobility industry, as well as some of the latest initiatives and strategies put in place in cities around the world to improve mobility and transportation. We have seen that changing preferences and technological breakthroughs are advancing old-style ways of managing urban mobility and also changing classical business models. However, despite developing alternatives to the automobile, cars are still very much an important mode of mobility for people around the world and will continue to be for a while.

Yet the global automobile industry is also experiencing groundbreaking transformations, due to technological advances and shifts in social attitudes and preferences. Figure 13 summarizes three of the latest changing forces or megatrends that will likely determine the future of urban automotive transportation and mobility: sharing mobility services, autonomous vehicles (AVs) and electric vehicles (EVs). The extent to which these three megatrends will converge in the future remains uncertain.

Figure 13: Future trends in urban automotive mobility

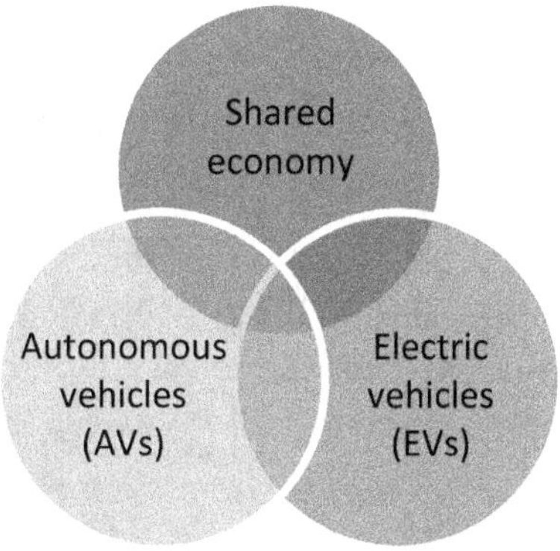

Source: Based on Shaheen (2015)

In previous sections, we discussed how the sharing economy and electric vehicles are entering the urban mobility game. We will next examine how autonomous vehicles are slowly advancing and are likely to become a reality very soon.

a. Autonomous vehicles (AVs)

Autonomous vehicles (AVs) are not as far-fetched as many people think and could be a reality in the near future. Recent innovations in the automotive industry and technological breakthroughs are paving the way for their introduction. AVs may be feasible sooner than expected, as various companies continue to make breakthroughs in the field. For instance, Google has said it plans to launch an autonomous car by 2020 and Uber is working together with the Carnegie Mellon University to create the Uber Advanced Technologies Center, with the aim of building AVs for use in its fleets (Bouton, et al., 2015).

If fully autonomous vehicles or driverless cars become a reality, they could significantly reduce many car-related negative effects and change the structure of car ownership. First, by linking AVs and car-pooling, the number of cars on the road could be reduced, leading to numerous benefits. For example, this could increase the carrying capacity of road infrastructures, reduce emissions and free up parking spaces (Bouton, et al., 2015; Harrold, 2015). Second, according to some preliminary estimates, AVs could cut accidents by up to 90%, by reducing the human factor behind the wheel (Bouton, et al., 2015). And third, AVs could lower the cost of personal mobility by 30% to 60% in relative terms to private automobile ownership (Bouton, et al., 2015). However, the main obstacle for self-driving cars will be regulation, which will pose important challenges.

Additionally, many experts believe that the future of car transportation lies not only in a vehicle that drives itself, but one that uses clean energy. With this in mind, companies such as Apple, Tesla, Google and Ford have declared the goal of developing their own electric autonomous vehicles (Eddy, 2016; Hepler, 2015). **The next generation of cars may be one that unites the three trends exhibited in Figure 13: electric autonomous cars that employ car-sharing schemes.**

***

4. Concluding Remarks

Urban mobility and transportation can contribute significantly to the economic and social development of cities, as well as to people's quality of life and health. However, current urbanization rates, alongside rising incomes per capita, will lead to increasing demand for mobility and transportation in cities. This growing pressure has spurred critical problems: currently, the world's transportation systems and infrastructures are overstressed; streets and highways are choked with traffic and congestion; road safety is at stake; environmental pressures are escalating; and rising air and noise pollution have sparked serious public health concerns.

Under a business-as-usual scenario, traditional ways of mobility in cities will not continue to be sustainable much longer. City managers around the world, especially in rapidly growing cities in developing countries, are struggling to cope with this growing demand. It is no longer wise to ignore the complexity of urban mobility and relegate transportation policies to second place among various priorities. **Urban mobility planning should be at the core of any city's strategy**.

As addressed in this book, multiple solutions and strategies have been developed in recent decades to stimulate a change towards more sustainable and integrated urban mobility systems. So far, many of these solutions are still "vertical solutions," but further integration is expected to take place. It has been shown that **the mobility and transportation sector is currently undergoing a paradigm shift**, with new alternatives to the automobile; changes in terms of energy use (clean energy, electrification and energy efficiency); new digital and applied technologies (transport demand management, integrated connectivity solutions and integrated inter-modal transportation); new business models and alternative ownership models (sharing economy); and shifts in people's behavior and preferences (on-demand services, real-time information, etc.). However, some of the new solutions, such as ride-sharing schemes or AVs, are facing regulatory challenges to their new business models and it is not clear how they will develop in the future.

Solving current urban mobility challenges will not be easy. Changing the existing mobility patterns will require huge investments in new infrastructures, and/or rehabilitating current ones, in public transport and the development of new and multi-modal transportation choices. Taking into account the financial constraints of local governments, coordinated actions with different stakeholders through different forms of Public-Private Partnerships (PPPs) have the potential to introduce efficiencies in the urban transport sector, offering alternative options for large projects and stimulating innovations. Collaboration in this new mobility economy will be essential.

Planners and city managers have a crucial role to play in this regard. Actions in the mobility and transportation sector are often more effective at the city level where policymakers are closer to their citizens and where they can design custom-made policies and schemes that better fit their local realities. **Sustainable urban mobility policies require a political vision and strategic thinking, careful planning, huge investments and strong urban transport governance.** If mobility schemes are not properly managed, they can result in a number of challenges with a direct effect on the quality of life of citizens. But if policies for urban mobility planning are well designed, so that they promote compact, transit-oriented and sustainable urban mobility systems, they can enhance accessibility, reduce air and noise pollution and

CO_2 emissions, ensure equitable access to all (poor, old, disabled, etc.) and offer more and cleaner modes of transportation.

Choices made in cities today about mobility and transportation will affect the sustainability of the urban areas of tomorrow and the behavior of the people who live in them. We believe that **the current paradigm shift in mobility and transportation is giving rise to the next generation of urban mobility, with more on-demand systems; more multi-modal services; more sharing mobility schemes; major improvements; important efficiency gains and enhancement in people's quality of life.**

5. References

Autolib (2015). "Autolib: An Urban Revolution", from https://www.autolib.eu/en/our-commitment/urban-revolution/

Berrone, P., Ricart, J.-E. and Duch T-Figueras, A. I. (2016). *Cities and the Environment: The challenge of becoming green and sustainable*. CreateSpace.

Bouton, S., Knupfer, S. M., Mihov, I., and Swartz, S. (2015). *Urban Mobility at a Tipping Point*. McKinsey & Company.

Breithaupt, M. (2015). *How to Make the Shift Towards Sustainable UrbanTtransport Modes Happen? Urban planning, Public transport, NMT and modal integration*. Presentation: GIZ - Water, Energy, Transport. Retrieved from https://www.iea.org/media/training/presentations/etw2015/transportpresentations/transport3/D.6.2_Making_sustainable_transport_happen.pdf

BRT Data (2016, 23 May 2016). "Global BRT Data", from http://brtdata.org/

Cebr (2014). *The Future Economic and Environmental Costs of Gridlock in 2030*. London: Centre for Economics and Business Research. Retrieved from http://www.greenfo.hu/uploads/dokumentumtar/inrixcosts-of-congestioncebr-report.pdf

Christensen, M. (2013). "Bike Share Statistics", from http://bikeshare.com/

City of Vienna (2015). "Smart City Wien - SMILE", from https://smartcity.wien.gv.at/site/en/projekte/verkehr-stadtentwicklung/smile-die-mobilitatsplattform-der-zukunft-2/

CIVITAS (2013). "Preparing a Congestion Charging Scheme: Stockholm", from http://www.civitas.eu/content/preparing-congestion-charging-scheme

Cohen, B., and Kietzmann, J. (2014). Ride On! Mobility Business Models for the Sharing Economy. *Organization & Environment, 27*, 279-296. doi: 10.1177/1086026614546199

Cornet, A., Mohr, D., Weig, F., Zerlin, B., and Hein, A.-P. (2012). *Mobility of the Future: Opportunities for Automotive OEMs.* Munich: McKinsey & Company, Inc.

Deloitte (2014). *Global Automotive Consumer Study - The Changing Nature of Mobility: Exploring Consumer Preferences in Key Markets Around the World.*

Dotter, F. (2015). *Car Sharing: New Forms of Vehicle Use and Ownership.* CIVITAS Insight n°5. Brussels: CIVITAS.

Earth Policy Institute (2013). Largest Bike-Sharing Programs Worldwide as of August 2013. Washington: Earth Policy Institute.

Earth Policy Institute (2015). Countries with Bike-Sharing Programs Dataset. Washington: Earth Policy Institute.

Eddy, N. (2016). Google, Tesla And Apple Race For Electric, Autonomous Vehicle Talent. Retrieved from http://www.informationweek.com/it-life/google-tesla-and-apple-race-for-electric-autonomous-vehicle-talent/d/d-id/1324351.

European Commission (2011). *Impact Assessment Accompanying the White Paper: Roadmap to a Single European Transport Area.* Brussels: European Commission.

Fang, W. (2014). "How Cities Can Save Trillions, Curb Climate Change, and Improve Public Health", from http://www.wri.org/blog/2014/09/how-cities-can-save-trillions-curb-climate-change-and-improve-public-health

Floater, G., and Rode, P. (2014). *Cities and the New Climate Economy: The Transformative Role of Global Urban Growth.*

Freese, C., and Schönberg, T. (2014). *Shared Mobility: How New Businesses Are Rewriting the Rules of the Private Transportation Game.* Think Act: Shared mobility. Market Study. Munich: Roland Berger Strategy Consultants GmbH.

Frost & Sullivan (2010). *Analysis of the Market for Carsharing in North America.* Market Research. Retrieved from http://www.frost.com/prod/servlet/report-overview.pag?repid=N748-01-00-00-00

Goodman, J., Laube, M., and Schwenk, J. (2007). Curitiba Bus System is Model for Rapid Transit. *Race, Poverty, and the Environment, 12.*

Harrold, P. (2015). "Driverless Cars: A Digital Future for the Automotive Aector". *Megatrends matters blog,* from http://pwc.blogs.com/megatrend_matters/2015/12/driverless-cars-a-digital-future-for-the-automotive-sector.html

Hawksworth, J., Hoehn, T., and Tiwari, A. (2009). *Which are the Largest City Economies in the World and How Might this Change by 2025?* PricewaterhouseCoopers UK Economic Outlook November 2009.

Hawksworth, J., and Vaughan, R. (2014). "The Sharing Economy – Sizing the Revenue Opportunity". *Megatrends - PricewaterhouseCoopers UK*, from http://www.pwc.co.uk/issues/megatrends/collisions/sharingeconomy/the-sharing-economy-sizing-the-revenue-opportunity.jhtml

Heinrichs, D., and Bernet, J. (2014). *Public Transport and Accessibility in Informal Settlements: Aeral Cable Cars in Medellin, Colombia*. Paper presented at the International Scientific Conference on Mobility and Transport - mobil. TUM 2014.

Hepler, L. (2015). Apple, Google, Tesla and the Race to Electric Self-driving Cars. Retrieved from https://www.greenbiz.com/article/apple-google-tesla-and-race-electric-self-driving-cars

Hidalgo, D., and Velasquez, J. M. (2015). "Mobility solutions for marginalized communities: The urban cable car", from http://thecityfix.com/blog/aerial-cable-cars-mobility-solutions-marginalized-communities-equity-dario-hidalgo-juan-miguel-velasquez/

Holguin-Veras, J., Ozbay, K., Kornhauser, A., Ukkusuri, S., Brom, M. A., Iyer, S., Yushimito, W. F., Allen, B., Silas, M. A. (2012). Overall Impacts of Off-Hour Delivery Programs in New York City Metropolitan Area: Lesson for European Cities. *Journal of the Transportation Research Board*.

Holguin-Veras, J., Wang, C., Browne, M., Hodge, S. D., and Wojtowicz, J. (2014). The New York City Off-hour Delivery Project: Lessons for City Logistics. *Procedia - Social and Behavioral Sciences, 125*(0), 36-48. doi: http://dx.doi.org/10.1016/j.sbspro.2014.01.1454

ITDP (2013). *The Bike-share Planning Guide*. New York: Institute for Transportation and Development Policy.

Johnston, C. (2014). Uber's Value More than Doubles to $40bn After Investors Back Fundraising. *The Guardian*. Retrieved from http://www.theguardian.com/technology/2014/dec/05/uber-value-doubles-after-fundraising

Jones, P. (2014). The Evolution of Urban Mobility: The Interplay of Academic and Policy Perspectives. *IATSS Research, 38*(1), 7-13. doi: http://dx.doi.org/10.1016/j.iatssr.2014.06.001

Kenworthy Jr. (2003). *Transport Energy Use and Greenhouse Gases in Urban Passenger Transport Systems: A Study of 84 Global Cities*. Paper presented at the International Third Conference of the Regional Government Network for Sustainable Development, Fremantle, Western Australia.

King, D. (2015). Frost & Sullivan expects 500,000 EVs to be sold worldwide in 2015. Retrieved from Autoblog website: http://www.autoblog.com/2015/02/19/frost-and-sullivan-expects-500-000-evs-to-be-sold-worldwide-in-201/

Lane, C., Zeng, H., Dhingra, C., and Carrigan, A. (2015). *Carsharing: A Vehicle For Sustainable Mobility In Emerging Markets?* Washington D.C.: World Resources Institute (WRI).

Leveque, F., and Moosa, M. (2013). "Voice of Future Car Sharing Customer: It's All about Wholly Sharing and Partly Pairing". *Frost & Sullivan Market Insight*, from http://www.frost.com/sublib/display-market-insight-top.do?id=273488817

Li, C. (2014). "From Ride-sharing to Taxi-hailing Apps: Here are 25 European Transportation Startups that Help You Get Around", from http://tech.eu/features/2501/european-transportation-startups-taxi-carsharing-ridesharing/

LTA Academy (2011). *Journeys: Sharing Urban Transport Solutions*. Singapore: LTA Academy, Land Transport Authority.

Manville, C., Cochrane, G., Cave, J., et al. (2014). *Mapping Smart Cities in the EU*. Brussels: European Parliament.

Mbeche, U. (2013). Sustainable urban mobility: visions beyond Europe. *Civitas Forum*. Brest: UN-Habitat.

Meddin, R. (2014). The Bike Sharing World - 2014.

Metro Medellin (2014). "Datos del Sistema", from https://www.metrodemedellin.gov.co/portals/4/Images/viajeconnosotros/infografico.jpg

MetroBike LLC (2015). "The Bike-sharing Blog", from http://bike-sharing.blogspot.com.es/

Midgley, P. (2011). *Bicycle-sharing schemes: enhancing sustainable mobility in urban areas*. Paper presented at the Commission on Sustainable Development, New York.

Mooney, C. (2015). To Truly Grasp What We're Doing to the Planet, You Need to Understand This Gigantic Measurement. *The Washington Post*. Retrieved from https://www.washingtonpost.com/news/energy-environment/wp/2015/07/01/meet-the-gigaton-the-huge-unit-that-scientists-use-to-track-planetary-change/

Mullaney, M. (2013). "Off-Hour Truck Deliveries in Manhattan Reduce Traffic, Empower Business Owners", from http://news.rpi.edu/content/2013/09/16/hour-truck-deliveries-manhattan-reduce-traffic-empower-business-owners#sthash.CJhqsEOu.dpuf

Navigant Research (2013). *Carsharing Membership and Vehicle Fleets, Personal Vehicle Reduction, and Revenue from Carsharing Services: Global Market Analysis and Forecasts*.

Navigant Research (2015). *Smart Parking Systems Sensor and Communications Hardware, Software, Services, and Smart City Applications: Global Market Analysis and Forecasts*. Retrieved from http://www.navigantresearch.com/research/smart-parking-systems

New Climate Economy (2014). *Better Growth , Better Climate: The New Climate Economy Report*. Washington D.C.: The Global Commission on the Economy and Climate. Retrieved from http://newclimateeconomy.report/

OECD/IEA (2012). *EV City Casebook: a look at the global electric vehicle movement*. Paris: Organisation for Economic Cooperation and Development/International Energy Agency.

P2P Foundation (2015). "Carsharing definition", from http://p2pfoundation.net/Carsharing

Papernick, H. (2015). Ride-Hailing VS Ride-Sharing – What's the Difference? Retrieved from https://blancride.com/blog/ride-hailing-vs-ride-sharing-whats-the-difference/

Picco, A. (2014). The OCTOPUS system - Contactless smart cards - Hong Kong. from Eltis http://www.eltis.org/discover/case-studies/octopus-system-contactless-smart-cards-hong-kong#sthash.taGxGmBR.dpuf

Replogle, M. (2014). "A Global High Shift to Public Transport, Walking, and Cycling: New Roadmap for Low Carbon Inclusive Urban Transportation", from https://www.itdp.org/a-global-high-shift-to-public-transport-walking-and-cycling-new-roadmap-for-low-carbon-inclusive-urban-transportation/

Rode, P., Floater, G., Thomopoulos, N., Docherty, J., Schwinger, P., Mahendra, A., and Fang, W. (2014). *Accessibility in cities: Transport and Urban Form*. NCE Cities Paper 03. LSE Cities: London School of Economics and Political Science.

Sandow, E. (2011). *On the Road : Social Aspects of Commuting Long Distances to Work*. Umeå University, Umeå.

Savy, M. (2012). Urban Freight: A Comprehensive Approach *Urban Freight for Livable Cities*. Göteborg: The Volvo Research and Educational Foundations, VREF.

SFpark, and SFMTA (2014). *SFpark: Pilot Project Evaluation Summary*. Retrieved from http://sfpark.org/wp-content/uploads/2014/06/SFpark_Eval_Summary_2014.pdf

Shaheen, S. (2015). Mobility + Sharing Economy: Past, Present and Future. Keynote Speech, June 5, 2015. *International Sharing Economy Symposium*. Utrecht, The Netherlands

Shaheen, S. A., Zhang, H., Martin, E., and Guzman, S. (2011). China's Hangzhou Public Bicycle. *Journal of the Transportation Research Board, 2247*, 33-41. doi: 10.3141/2247-05

Shoup, D. C. (2006). Cruising for Parking. *Transport Policy, 13*(6), 479–486. doi: 10.1016/j.tranpol.2006.05.005

Statistics South Africa (2011). "City of Johannesburg: Key Statistics", from http://www.statssa.gov.za/?page_id=1021&id=city-of-johannesburg-municipality

Stockholm Business Region (2013). Facts about Business in Stockholm 2013. Retrieved from http://www.stockholmbusinessregion.se/Global/About%20Us/Publikationer/Facts%20about%20business.pdf

Thomson, I., and Bull, A. (2002). Urban Traffic Congestion: Its Economic and Social Causes and Consequences. *CEPAL Review, 76*, 105-116.

Thorpe, D. (2015). Dubai Becomes First City to Fuel Municipal Vehicles on 100% Local Waste Cooking Oil. Retrieved from http://www.sustainablecitiescollective.com/david-thorpe/1042981/dubai-becomes-first-city-fuel-municipal-vehicles-100-local-waste-cooking-oil

TomTom International BV (2016). "TomTom Traffic Index: Measuring congestion worldwide", from http://www.tomtom.com/en_gb/trafficindex/#/

Tools of Change (2014). "Stockholm Congestion Pricing", from http://www.toolsofchange.com/en/case-studies/detail/670.

Townsend, A. M. (2014). *Smart Cities: Big Data, Civic Hackers, and the Quest for a New Utopia* (1 ed.). New York: W. W. Norton & Company.

UITP (2009). *Public Transport and CO2 emissions*. Brussels: UITP (International Association of Public Transport).

UITP (2012). "How Will Our Cities look in 2025?". *Grow with Public Transportation*, from http://growpublictransport.org/wp-content/uploads/2013/02/Scenarios_PDF_new_13.02.06.pdf

UITP (2014). Statistics Brief: *World Metro Figures*. Brussels: UITP.

UITP (2015a). *Mobility in Cities Database: Synthesis Report*. Retrieved from http://www.uitp.org/sites/default/files/cck-focus-papers-files/MCD_2015_synthesis_web.pdf

UITP (2015b). *Public Transport Trends 2015*.

UN-Habitat (2010). *State of the World's Cities 2010/2011: Bridging the Urban Divide*. Nairobi: United Nations Human Settlements Programme (UN-HABITAT).

UN-Habitat (2013). *Planning and Design for Sustainable Urban Mobility: Policy Directions.* Global Report on Human Settlements 2013. Nairobi: UN-Habitat.

UN (United Nations) (2013). *World Economic and Social Survey 2013: Sustainable Development Challenges.* New York: United Nations.

UN (United Nations) (2014). *Transport: International Association of Public Transport Action Plan.* Paper presented at the Climate Summit 2014, New York.

UNCSD (2012). *Rio 2012 Issues Briefs: Sustainable, Low Carbon Transport in Emerging and Developing Economies.* Paper presented at the Rio+20 United Nations Conference on Sustainable Development.

University of California - Davis (2014). Global Shift Away from Cars Would Save US$100 trillion, Eliminate 1,700 Megatons of Carbon Dioxide Pollution. *ScienceDaily.* Retrieved from https://www.sciencedaily.com/releases/2014/09/140917073300.htm

Urban ITS Expert Group (2013). *ITS Action Plan – Best Practices: Collection of projects.*

US Department of transportation, NYC, and Rensselaer Polytechnic Institute (2013). NYC deliverEASE Off-Hour. On Time - Participant Packet. Retrieved from https://www.tfl.gov.uk/cdn/static/cms/documents/nyc-off-hours-trial-participant-pack.pdf

Van-Audenhove, F.-J., DeJongh, S., and Durance, M. (2015). *Urban Logistics: How to Unlock Value from Last Mile Delivery for Cities, Transporters and Retailers.* Brussels: Arthur D. Little.

Van-Audenhove, F.-J., Korniichuk, O., Dauby, L., and Pourbaix, J. (2014). *The Future of Urban Mobility 2.0: Imperatives to Shape Extended Mobility Ecosystems of Tomorrow.* Brussels: Arthur D. Little and UITP.

Vaz, E., and Venter, C. (2012). *The Effectiveness of Bus Rapid Transit as Part of Poverty-reduction Strategy: Some Early Impacts in Johannesburg.* Paper presented at the 31st Southern African Transport Conference, Pretoria. http://repository.up.ac.za/bitstream/handle/2263/20221/Vaz_Effectiveness%282012%29.pdf?sequence=3

WHO (World Health Organization) (2013). *Global Status Report on Road Safety 2013: Supporting a Decade of Action.* Luxembourg: World Health Organization.

WHO (World Health Organization) (2014). "7 Million Premature Deaths Annually Linked to Air Pollution", from http://www.who.int/mediacentre/news/releases/2014/air-pollution/en/

Wilson, S. (2012). Stockholm Congestion Pricing Has Had Long-Term Effects on Traffic Levels. Retrieved from http://roadpricing.blogspot.com.es.

World Bank (2002). *Cities on the Move : A World Bank Urban Transport Strategy Review*. Washington, DC: The World Bank.

World Bank (2011). "Case Studies: Johannesburg, South Africa". *Toolkit on Intelligent Transport Systems for Urban Transport*, from http://www.ssatp.org/sites/ssatp/files/publications/Toolkits/ITS%20Toolkit%20content/case-studies/johannesburg-south-africa.html

World Bank (2012). "Cairo Traffic is Much More than a Nuisance", from http://www.worldbank.org/en/news/feature/2012/08/21/cairo-traffic-much-more-than-nuisance

World Cities Culture Forum (2016). "Cities: Paris", from http://www.worldcitiescultureforum.com/cities/paris

Xerox (2014). "To the Moon and Back: In Search of Smart Parking", from http://www.washingtonpost.com/sf/brand-connect/wp/enterprise/to-the-moon-and-back-in-search-of-smart-parking/

Zenghelis, D., and Stern, N. (2015). Climate Change and Cities: A Prime Source of Problems, Yet Key to a Solution, *The Guardian*. Retrieved from http://www.theguardian.com/cities/2015/nov/17/cities-climate-change-problems-solution

Zhang, R. (2014). Autonomous Mobility-On-Demand – A Solution for Sustainable Urban Personal Mobility. *Stanford Energy Journal* (Issue 4: Sustainable Transportation).

6. Appendix I: Additional Resources

On the IESE Cities in Motion Strategies website you will find additional related material and resources. Check the following link regularly to access our latest publications:

• IESE Cities in Motion Strategies: http://www.iese.edu/cim.

Additionally, the authors recommend the following Internet resources for more information on the topic:

• C40 Cities – http://www.c40.org.
• Cities for Mobility (CfM) - http://www.cities-for-mobility.net.
• CityLab - http://www.citylab.com.
• Citymapper - https://citymapper.com.
• CIVITAS Initiative - http://www.civitas.eu.
• EcoMobility - http://ecomobility.org.
• Eltis: The urban mobility observatory - http://www.eltis.org.
• ENCLOSE (Energy efficiency in City Logistics Services) - http://www.enclose.eu.
• EUROCITIES - http://www.eurocities.eu.
• GIZ Sustainable Urban Transport Project - http://www.sutp.org.
• Grow Smarter - http://www.grow-smarter.eu.
• ICLEI-Local Governments for Sustainability - http://www.iclei.org.
• Institute for Transport and Development Policy (ITDP) - https://www.itdp.org.
• International Road Traffic and Accident Database (IRTAD) - http://www.internationaltransportforum.org.

- Leading Cities - http://leadingcities.org.
- Metropolis - http://www.metropolis.org.
- Mobility & Trends - http://www.mobility-trends.com.
- Moovit - http://moovitapp.com.
- New Cities Foundation - http://www.newcitiesfoundation.org.
- New Mobility World - http://newmobilityworld.com.
- OECD – Urban Development - http://www.oecd.org/regional/regional-policy/urbandevelopment.htm.
- POLIS Network - http://www.polisnetwork.eu.
- Smart Cities Council - http://smartcitiescouncil.com.
- UN-Habitat - http://unhabitat.org.
- UN-World Urbanization Prospects -http://esa.un.org/unpd/wup.
- UITP: Advancing Public Transport - http://www.uitp.org.
- Waze - https://www.waze.com.
- World Bank - http://www.worldbank.org.
- World Health Organization (WHO) – http://www.who.int.
- WRI Ross Center for Sustainable Cities - http://www.wricities.org.

7. Appendix II: Cities in Motion Index – Mobility and Transportation Dimension

This appendix includes a brief presentation of the IESE Cities in Motion Index, focusing on the mobility and transportation dimension. For more information on the index, please check the IESE Cities in Motion website www.iese.edu/cim, with all our latest publications.

CITIES IN MOTION INDEX

The Cities in Motion Index (CIMI) has been designed with the aim of constructing a "breakthrough" indicator in terms of its completeness, characteristics, comparability and the quality and objectivity of its information. Its goal is to enable measurement of the future sustainability of the world's main cities as well as the quality of life of their inhabitants.

The CIMI aims to help the public and governments to understand the performance of 10 fundamental dimensions for a city: governance, urban planning, public management, technology, the environment, international outreach, social cohesion, mobility and transportation, human capital, and the economy. Thanks to its broad and integrated vision of the city, the Cities in Motion Index enables to recognize the strengths and weaknesses of each city, allowing to identify effective solutions.

The 2016 edition is the third consecutive CIMI, covering the years 2013, 2014 and 2015. It includes a total of 181 cities, of which 72 are capitals representing more than 80 different countries, as well as 77 indicators measuring the 10 relevant dimensions.

RANKING *CIMI* 2015

New York City (United States) is in first place in the overall ranking, driven by its performance in the dimensions of the economy (first place), technology (third place) and in human capital, public management, governance, international outreach, and mobility and transportation (fourth place). However, for another year, it continues to be in very low positions in the dimensions of social cohesion (position 161) and in environment (position 93). Following New York, we find London (UK) in the second place of the ranking and Paris (France) in the third place.

Of the 10 top positions of the ranking, four cities are in the U.S. (New York, San Francisco, Boston and Chicago); four cities are in Europe (London, Paris, Amsterdam and Geneva); one is in Asia (Seoul) and one in Oceania (Sydney).

TABLE A1. CITY RANKING. TOP 10

CIMI 2015	City (Country)
1	New York City (United States)
2	London (United Kingdom)
3	Paris (France)
4	San Francisco (United States)
5	Boston (United States)
6	Amsterdam (Netherlands)
7	Chicago (United States)

8	Seoul (South Korea)
9	Geneva (Switzerland)
10	Sydney (Australia)

DIMENSION: MOBILITY AND TRANSPORTATION

The cities of the future have to tackle two major challenges in the field of mobility and transportation: facilitating movement through cities (often large ones) and facilitating access to public services.

Mobility and transportation – with regard to road and route infrastructure, the vehicle fleet and public transportation, and to air transportation – affect the quality of life of a city's inhabitants and can be vital to the sustainability of cities over time. However, perhaps the most important aspect is the externalities that are generated in the production system, both because of the workforce's need to commute and because of the need for an outlet for production.

Table A2 sets out the indicators selected in the dimension of mobility and transportation, descriptions of them, their units of measurement and the sources of information.

TABLE A2. MOBILITY AND TRANSPORTATION INDICATORS

Indicator	Description / Unit of measurement	Source
Traffic index	The traffic index is estimated by considering the time spent in traffic and the dissatisfaction this generates. It also includes estimates of CO_2 consumption and the other inefficiencies of the traffic system	Numbeo
Inefficiency index	The inefficiency index is an estimate of the inefficiencies in traffic. High values represent high rates of inefficiency in driving, such as long journey times	Numbeo

Number of road accidents	Number of road accidents per 100,000 inhabitants	Euromonitor
Metro	Number of metro stations per city	2thinknow
Flights	Number of arrival and departure flights (air routes) in a city	2thinknow
Means of transportation	The means of transportation represents the public transportation options for smart cities. The value of the variable increases if there are more transportation options. The lack of transportation options can make a city less attractive as a smart destination	2thinknow
Index of traffic for commuting to work	Index of traffic considering the journey time to work	Numbeo

The general traffic index, the index of traffic caused by commuting to work, and the inefficiency index are estimates of the traffic inefficiencies caused by long driving times and by the dissatisfaction that these situations generate in the population. These indicators, along with the number of road accidents, are a measure of the efficiency and safety of roads and public transportation, which, if it is effective and has good infrastructure, promotes a decrease in vehicular traffic on the roads and reduces the number of accidents. All these are included with a negative sign in the calculation of the CIMI, since they have a negative impact on the development of a sustainable city.

In turn, the number of metro stations is an indicator of commitment to the development of the city and investment with respect to the population size. The means of transportation represent the public transportation options of a city. The value of this variable increases if there are more transportation options. The lack of transportation options can reduce the attractiveness of a city as a smart destination. The number of air routes (arrivals and departures) that a city has represents the infrastructure that it has to facilitate commercial air routes and, therefore, passenger circulation and transit. These three indicators are included with a positive sign because of the positive influence they have on the dimension.

RANKING – MOBILITY AND TRANSPORTATION DIMENSION

In the mobility and transportation dimension, the city of Seoul (South Korea) comes first in the ranking and stands out in almost all the indicators. Of the top 10 cities in the ranking for this dimension, there are seven European cities.

TABLE A3. RANKING BY DIMENSION: MOBILITY AND TRANSPORTATION

City, Country	Mobility and Transportation Ranking	CIMI 2015 Ranking
Seoul, South Korea	1	8
Frankfurt, Germany	2	35
London, United Kingdom	3	2
New York City, United States	4	1
Madrid, Spain	5	34
Paris, France	6	3
Zurich, Switzerland	7	14
Vienna, Austria	8	26
Beijing, China	9	92
Barcelona, Spain	10	33
Stockholm, Sweden	11	27
Shanghai, China	12	93
Singapore, Singapore	13	22
Munich, Germany	14	21

City, Country	Mobility and Transportation Ranking	CIMI 2015 Ranking
Boston, United States	15	5
Berlin, Germany	16	16
Chicago, United States	17	7
Guangzhou, China	18	104
Oslo, Norway	19	28
Amsterdam, Netherlands	20	6
Brussels, Belgium	21	32
Sydney, Australia	22	10
Philadelphia, United States	23	23
Los Angeles, United States	24	15
Helsinki, Finland	25	25
Moscow, Russia	26	108
San Francisco, United States	27	4
Dallas, United States	28	19
Manchester, United Kingdom	29	43
Copenhagen, Denmark	30	11
Prague, Czech Republic	31	45
Istanbul, Turkey	32	109
Melbourne, Australia	33	17
Tokyo, Japan	34	12
Hamburg, Germany	35	41
Budapest, Hungary	36	68
Shenzhen, China	37	130
Mexico City, Mexico	38	100
Stuttgart, Germany	39	51
Chongqing, China	40	147
Kiev, Ukraine	41	143
Toronto, Canada	42	24

City, Country	Mobility and Transportation Ranking	CIMI 2015 Ranking
Dubai, United Arab Emirates	43	65
Lisbon, Portugal	44	62
Naples, Italy	45	90
Dublin, Ireland	46	36
Valencia, Spain	47	49
Wuhan, China	48	153
Baltimore, United States	49	18
Porto, Portugal	50	76
Auckland, New Zealand	51	29
Brasilia, Brazil	52	136
Taipei, Taiwan	53	64
Osaka, Japan	54	56
Tallinn, Estonia	55	54
Malaga, Spain	56	58
Milan, Italy	57	44
Delhi, India	58	174
Cologne, Germany	59	52
Kuala Lumpur, Malaysia	60	88
Warsaw, Poland	61	74
Busan, South Korea	62	91
Athens, Greece	63	113
Monterrey, Mexico	64	102
Geneva, Switzerland	65	9
Basel, Switzerland	66	42
Turin, Italy	67	82
Abu Dhabi, United Arab Emirates	68	66
Lyon, France	69	55
Almaty, Kazakhstan	70	125

City, Country	Mobility and Transportation Ranking	CIMI 2015 Ranking
Riga, Latvia	71	78
Bangkok, Thailand	72	84
Sao Paulo, Brazil	73	124
Buenos Aires, Argentina	74	85
Bilbao, Spain	75	69
Duisburg, Germany	76	73
Marseille, France	77	72
Belgrade, Serbia	78	114
Liverpool, United Kingdom	79	48
Birmingham, United Kingdom	80	47
Phoenix, United States	81	40
Vancouver, Canada	82	20
Medellin, Colombia	83	99
Nice, France	84	61
Miami, United States	85	53
Rome, Italy	86	81
Ankara, Turkey	87	127
Gothenburg, Sweden	88	57
Seville, Spain	89	67
Bursa, Turkey	90	128
Caracas, Venezuela	91	162
Hong Kong, China	92	39
Rio de Janeiro, Brazil	93	139
Saint Petersburg, Russia	94	133
Nottingham, United Kingdom	95	75
Tianjin, China	96	166
Shenyang, China	97	155
Doha, Qatar	98	117

City, Country	Mobility and Transportation Ranking	CIMI 2015 Ranking
Kaohsiung, Taiwan	99	103
Bucharest, Romania	100	110
Guadalajara, Mexico	101	116
Glasgow, United Kingdom	102	46
Ljubljana, Slovenia	103	86
Haifa, Israel	104	101
Florence, Italy	105	50
Santiago, Chile	106	80
Minsk, Belarus	107	137
Sofia, Bulgaria	108	95
Linz, Austria	109	63
Nagoya, Japan	110	87
Lima, Peru	111	122
Jidda, Saudi Arabia	112	115
Daegu, South Korea	113	98
Douala, Cameroon	114	175
Porto Alegre, Brazil	115	118
Bratislava, Slovakia	116	83
Houston, United States	117	31
A Coruna, Spain	118	60
Ottawa, Canada	119	30
Rotterdam, Netherlands	120	70
Vilnius, Lithuania	121	89
San Jose, Costa Rica	122	131
Daejeon, South Korea	123	96
Tbilisi, Georgia	124	135
Montreal, Canada	125	38
Wroclaw, Poland	126	94

City, Country	Mobility and Transportation Ranking	CIMI 2015 Ranking
Leeds, United Kingdom	127	71
Zagreb, Croatia	128	107
Manila, Philippines	129	145
Ho Chi Minh City, Vietnam	130	158
Cairo, Egypt	131	156
London, Canada	132	37
Lille, France	133	79
Suzhou, China	134	165
Antwerp, Belgium	135	77
Bombay, India	136	167
Quito, Ecuador	137	132
Casablanca, Morocco	138	163
Tehran, Iran	139	177
Taichung, Taiwan	140	112
Baku, Azerbaijan	141	150
Harbin, China	142	169
Tel Aviv, Israel	143	97
Santo Domingo, Dominican Republic	144	172
Johannesburg, South Africa	145	140
Jakarta, Indonesia	146	170
Bogota, Colombia	147	111
Tunis, Tunisia	148	144
Cordoba, Argentina	149	106
Rosario, Argentina	150	134
Jerusalem, Israel	151	105
Fortaleza, Brazil	152	149
Tainan, Taiwan	153	141
Washington, D.C., United States	154	13

City, Country	Mobility and Transportation Ranking	CIMI 2015 Ranking
Curitiba, Brazil	155	129
Novosibirsk, Russia	156	154
Karachi, Pakistan	157	181
Santa Cruz, Bolivia	158	171
Eindhoven, Netherlands	159	59
Alexandria, Egypt	160	173
Salvador, Brazil	161	151
Cape Town, South Africa	162	120
Bangalore, India	163	176
Nairobi, Kenya	164	178
Lagos, Nigeria	165	180
Belo Horizonte, Brazil	166	152
Amman, Jordan	167	160
Sarajevo, Bosnia and Herzegovina	168	157
Guatemala City, Guatemala	169	161
Cali, Colombia	170	126
La Paz, Bolivia	171	168
Montevideo, Uruguay	172	121
Durban, South Africa	173	159
Guayaquil, Ecuador	174	148
Skopje, Macedonia	175	146
Kuwait, Kuwait	176	119
Recife, Brazil	177	142
Pretoria, South Africa	178	164
Riyadh, Saudi Arabia	179	123
Manama, Bahrein	180	138
Kolkata, India	181	179

www.ingramcontent.com/pod-product-compliance
Lightning Source LLC
Chambersburg PA
CBHW071821200526
45169CB00018B/549